THE PROBLEM
of BLACK SKIN

THE PROBLEM
of BLACK SKIN

Critical Reflections on Cultural Awareness,
Social Change, and Spiritual Evolution

DeWayne R. Stallworth

CASCADE *Books* • Eugene, Oregon

THE PROBLEM OF BLACK SKIN
Critical Reflections on Cultural Awareness, Social Change, and Spiritual Evolution

Copyright © 2025 DeWayne R. Stallworth. All rights reserved. Except for brief quotations in critical publications or reviews, no part of this book may be reproduced in any manner without prior written permission from the publisher. Write: Permissions, Wipf and Stock Publishers, 199 W. 8th Ave., Suite 3, Eugene, OR 97401.

Cascade Books
An Imprint of Wipf and Stock Publishers
199 W. 8th Ave., Suite 3
Eugene, OR 97401

www.wipfandstock.com

PAPERBACK ISBN: 979-8-3852-2579-8
HARDCOVER ISBN: 979-8-3852-2580-4
EBOOK ISBN: 979-8-3852-2581-1

Cataloguing-in-Publication data:

Names: Stallworth, DeWayne R., author.

Title: The problem of black skin : critical reflections on cultural awareness, social change, and spiritual evolution / DeWayne R. Stallworth.

Description: Eugene, OR : Cascade Books, 2025 | Includes bibliographical references and index.

Identifiers: ISBN 979-8-3852-2579-8 (paperback) | ISBN 979-8-3852-2580-4 (hardcover) | ISBN 979-8-3852-2581-1 (ebook)

Subjects: LCSH: Black race—Social conditions. | Black race—Psychology. | Race relations. Racism.| Human skin color. | Human skin color—Social aspects. | African Americans—Religion. | Spirituality—United States.

Classification: BR563.B53 .S72 2025 (paperback) | BR563.B53 .S72 (ebook)

VERSION NUMBER 032725

This book is dedicated to the students, scholars, and social change advocates of the *New, New World*.

CONTENTS

THE FORETHOUGHT
A Reflection on Anti-Blackness
(*Dirty Black Hand and Cultural Criticism*) | 1

1. A MYTH OF BLACKNESS (*We Come from the Stars*) | 12
2. IGNORANCE, ARROGANCE, AND THE *THING* | 26
3. BETWEEN A ROCK AND A HARD PLACE
   (*The Origin of Black Compromise and Betrayal*) | 37
4. TOWARD A *NEW WORLD*
   (*Pawns of Commerce and the New Enterprise of Chattel Slavery*) | 48
5. THE SLAVE SHIP EXPERIENCE (*A Beautiful Struggle*) | 58
6. PRESSING FORWARD/PRESSED BACKWARD
   (*The Spirit of Black Progression and Black Privilege*) | 65
7. THE LEGITIMATION OF WHITENESS
   (*The Du Boisian Entanglement of Religion, Morality, and Society*) | 76
8. A CULTURAL PARADOX: The "Traditional" Black Church
   (*Spirits of Rebellion and Abandonment*) | 92
9. THE ESSENCE OF THE MATTER (*The Thing*) | 107

AFTERTHOUGHT
A Way Out of This Mess (*Spirituality and the Divine Spark Within*) | 125

Bibliography | 133
Index | 145

THE FORETHOUGHT
A Reflection on Anti-Blackness
(*Dirty Black Hand and Cultural Criticism*)

I CAN REMEMBER THE precise moment I began the process of understanding that black skin presented as a problem to the social world around me. I was ten and attending a predominately white elementary school in the Deep South. If memory serves me correctly, it was a pleasant day. The weather was mildly warm, and the sky a light blue hue. Students were taking a break, and most boys sat at a table, as most boys did in the 1990s, and began displaying and trading their sports cards. I was the only black who gathered in this group. Four white boys sat in the chairs as they vigorously argued the value of each of their respective cards. As negotiations intensified, the white boy on my right wielded a much-coveted Michael Jordan basketball card before the group. Because I had never held such a prized item, I confidently extended my hand and tried to pick up the card for a more detailed and intimate observation. What happened next left me, to say the very least, stunned, shocked, and mortified.

As I tried to grab the card and lift it from the table, the white boy on my right side slapped my hand and forcefully shouted, "*You better get your dirty black hands off my stuff!*" Every white boy at the table laughed as they continued to negotiate terms. I, on the other hand, did not find such a gesture amusing. I faded from the scene and stood alone as I processed the degree to which I found myself looking at my hand and wondering why so much negative energy was placed on my black skin. How did a ten-year-old, I pondered, learn to categorize black and white skin significance? Analyzing such an experience with a sense of understanding would take years. But I learned a valuable lesson that day, no doubt. I could be around white people only if a limitation was associated with my black skin. Such a limitation, however, has never been appealing. The descriptive *dirty black hand* that my white classmate highlighted was a result of family conversations, religious affiliation, and peer relationships. Regardless of the formulation, at the tender age of ten, I learned that white children had been taught, both consciously and unconsciously, to believe that black skin meant something as *other* or void of certain human aspects. And if the need should arise, black skin should be physically restrained in the event racial lines were ever crossed.

According to current epigenetic research, behavior can be passed down to fourteen generations through familial and cultural DNA.[1] For argument's sake, let us presume that the white boys, especially the bold one who slapped my hand, learned that black skin had social limitations from their parents and grandparents; pressing a bit further, let us presume that the parents and grandparents learned it from their parents and grandparents and so on. This generational trajectory places the origin of the problem of black skin in America within the mid-sixteenth century, as outlined in Winthrop Jordan's classic *White over Black*. Thus, at both conscious and unconscious levels, the laughter, disrespect, and physical aggression displayed that day by my white peers were the result of a centuries-old cultural inheritance that defines black skin as socially and culturally problematic.

THE PROBLEM
(A Sketch of Black Skin)

Due to the longevity of the problem of black skin, opinion varies on just how much attention should be placed on historical reflection and the overall significance chattel enslavement had on present-day cultural norms. Some would suggest that although slavery was a horrific experience in what is deemed as the American experiment and that earlier generations of blacks indeed faced tremendous opposition to social elevation, progress has nevertheless been made. Furthermore, a comparative analysis would prove that the twenty-first-century black person has more opportunities to succeed than the twentieth-century black person. Such a position could entail an awareness of just how entrenched racism is in America; therefore, as the argument goes, it is absurd to believe that it is even probable to

---

1. See Yehuda, "How Parents' Trauma"; Breton et al., "Exploring the Evidence"; Kaneshiro et al., "Sperm-Inherited H3K27me3."

eradicate such entrenched racist tendencies from the fabric of American cultural norms. It, therefore, behooves blacks to take advantage of as many opportunities as possible and learn to be satisfied in a bubble of limited social security (however, it is seldom viewed and presented as such), and although there are still those whites who display their hatred of black skin through acts of aggression and violence, such individuals are in the minority; therefore, it is unreasonable to conclude that America is an inherently racist country.[2] I believe, however, that such opinions and positions lack validity when I consider the intricate influences that society, culture, and religion have on an individual; interestingly enough, these individuals collectively create norms that govern and guide society.

I argue that the notion of black skin, and the facets thereof, is a social tool designed to confer a particular group of people as a less desirable human design and worthy of social subjugation; additionally, the process of blackness created experiences that codifies a specific group of people with mutually inherited cultural antecedents. I desire to expose remnants of truth that could help explain how black skin would come to be detested and discover how we might address such an intricate problem known as black skin. Because of the complex and interrelated components of race construction, when I attempt to better understand what it means to have black skin in modern-day America, I frame the issue of black-skin *othering* from an intentional point of departure, with the crux of the weight being placed on English expeditions and colonization practices.

The English development of the North American continent began in earnest in the 1550s; in the so-called *New World* development, Sir John Hawkins, with the permission of Queen Elizabeth, sailed to Sierra Leone and stole Africans to trade in sugar, jewelry, and so on. Despite involvement

---

2. In Allport, *Nature of Prejudice,* one is introduced to five levels of disdain for black skin. First, there is anti-locution; words are the extent of one's disdain at this level of prejudice. The second is avoidance. One simply creates distance between self and the object of social ridicule. Such a one, for instance, would move if a black family relocated into their neighborhood as opposed to burning a cross in their yard or committing other acts of vandalism. Third is the act of discrimination. This level of prejudice is what fueled the Jim Crow era. A person with prejudice against black skin will actively look to implement policies, ordinances, customs, and laws as a means of disassociating from the societal engagement of equity and equality. Fourth, physical attack. This level of aggression toward black skin would usually manifest in warnings; for instance, homes, churches, and schools are firebombed as a way of alerting blacks to the fact that they are agitating the social structure of anti-blackness too much and too often. The fifth and last element in Allport's five-point scale is extermination.

by several European nations in the African slave trade, the English can be credited with establishing the colonies in North America, which benefited the most from the free labor and abundance of land and resource acquisition of *New World* chattel enslavement. It is important to note that in the sixteenth century, black skin had been socially ingrained in the European psyche to convey dirty, filthy, foul, and sinister essence. Whites had a fundamental notion of what was considered ideal and beautiful. Ideally, Africans failed the color and features (e.g., lips, nose, cheeks, and butt) test. Thus, their *otherness* (i.e., religion, dress, culture) became repulsive to European sensibilities. However, it is essential to note the hypocrisy associated with such an ideal. Enslaved African Sarah (Saartie) Baartman's body was both abused and idealized by many European men and women by the early 1800s. In Victorian Europe, women of the upper echelon of society wore the bustle. This fashion accessory afforded wealthy white women the privilege of expanding the perception of buttocks, which closely aligned to that naturally observed in Baartman's body structure. Europeans seem to have developed a dialectical relationship with the black body. On the one hand, black bodies such as Baartman's were considered deformed and outside the standard that governs genteel European sensibilities; on the other hand, bodies such as Baartman's were used for sexual pleasure, and I presume white women mimicked the black female bodily attributes in response to their gentlemen being lured away from the familial arms of fidelity.

By 1619, Jamestown, Virginia, became a distant home to, in the words of John Rolfe, "20 and odd negroes."[3] As European powers collided in efforts to set up sovereignty across the known world and its abundant supply of resources, the English vessel *White Lion* robbed the *San Juan Bautista*, and these Angolans legitimately became the forebears of the African American/black heritage. And by 1624, Anthony and Isabella gave birth to the first African American, William.

In 1640, the first inductee into the institution of American chattel enslavement occurred in Virginia when John Punch, a runaway servant, was given a life sentence. Conversely, a Dutchman and a Scot who also ran away were sentenced to serve only four more years (one each for their master and three for the colony). This is the essential historical pivot that promoted, in America, the ideal discrimination and differentiation of black skin as inherently subject to harsher treatment than white skin, even if both have been found guilty of breaking the same law of the land. After the official

---

3. Rolfe, "John Rolfe's Letter," 9.

end of American chattel enslavement, the so-called free black was left to exist in a country where skin color dictated levels of social elevation and worth.

The American English cultural inheritance of black-skin *hatred* intensified because of frustration at the integration of what many poor and wealthy whites considered to be an affront to white human decency. For instance, enslavers and some poor whites understood black freedom and social standing to equate to that of a dog, cattle, horse, or any other property obtaining its freedom and now having a share of social equality and rights of human citizenship. Unsurprisingly, such a perceived cultural affront would be met with violent resistance and resolve. After making such an abrupt cultural adaptation into an *equal* society, confused and enraged whites began setting up an official anti-black-skin agenda.

What has been termed anti-blackness by scholars and political pundits alike was well proven in America by the 1870s when whites refused to sell land to formerly enslaved people, a needed asset to survive in the nineteenth century. As noted in Rayford Logan's classic work *The Betrayal of the Negro* and W. E. B. Du Bois's *Black Reconstruction*, newly freed blacks enjoyed only seven years of economic and social freedom before the anti-black agenda went into full force. Additionally, the few blacks who managed to become landowners were intimidated and forced to yield to white demands of rightful ownership. Slave labor was replaced with a system of sharecropping, which was nothing more than debt entrapment, a perennial cycle on the wheel of social misfortune. The birth of anti-black groups such as the Ku Klux Klan, Red Shirts, Knights of the White Camelia, White Leagues, and the White Brotherhood placed high levels of intimidation on both black and white people who were possessed with the *black zeitgeist* (i.e., the spirit of black progression); the highest level of intimidation being murder. In 1871, for instance, Betsey Westbrook of Jefferson gave congressional testimony in Demopolis, Alabama, about the murder of her husband at the hands of hooded vigilantes. "They promised to kill him," she says, "and I knew they were going to kill him."[4] In the same month, Eliza Lyon, from Demopolis, gave testimony to the fact that her husband was killed by the Klan.[5]

---

4. See Alexander, *Reconstruction Violence*, 56–70.

5. My experience of the *dirty black hand* took place in the Deep South, Demopolis, Alabama.

THE PROBLEM OF BLACK SKIN

No doubt about it; the so-called Reconstruction era gave birth to Jim Crow (1877–1964) as well as Black Codes. Although the Civil Rights Act of 1875 granted blacks access to public accommodations, this tempered movement of progress was halted when the law was reversed in 1883. A hundred years would pass before this reversal would be addressed via additional legislation. By 1896, *Plessy v. Ferguson* made the social doctrine of America separate but equal. Indeed, Plessy provided the legal context for the *black zeitgeist* to continue the struggle for liberation through boycotts, marches, protests, and lobbying up until Dr. Martin Luther King Jr.'s assassination. Something peculiar happened to black life, and the world for that matter, when Dr. King was assassinated on April 4, 1968, in Memphis, Tennessee.

The man (i.e., Martin Luther King Jr.) who was killed in Memphis in 1968 was not the same man who led a successful Montgomery bus boycott in 1956. So much had happened. There were several attempted assassinations in his life. Public acceptance of his tactics and philosophy of nonresistance protest and social agitation had faded by 1968; at this time, Dr. King had seen how the desire for control and elevation had compromised both black and white spaces. Dr. King was undoubtedly well acquainted with the historical progression and significance of anti-blackness in America. Still, Dr. King had also intellectually matured into a person who, one must remember, understood the dynamics of race construction but also gained a greater awareness that anti-blackness was a symptom of a much larger disease. Anti-blackness for Dr. King was a matter that needed serious attention; however, it was not the *Thing*. Dr. King was not killed because of his stance against black-skin *othering* alone; just the opposite, Dr. King was killed primarily because he began agitating the *Thing* at a level of focus and intentionality that began frustrating some influential people. His resolve had the potential to help expose and effectively combat the *Thing*. Moreover, King's emphasis on love is crucial, for love is the ultimate weapon against anti-blackness and other forms of hate and evil.

When King employs the term "love," he does so with attention placed on a cosmic level. As King understood it, love is not derived from the mind and heart of human beings; instead, love is the functioning source that governs every essence in the known cosmos and is expressed via the mind and heart. Love is a creative force that has the potential to shift realities of inequality into new dimensions of unity and goodwill toward all of humanity. The key to unlocking this power, which can remedy the *Thing*, lies in spiritual awareness/consciousness, which is at the core of all individuals. Unfortunately, such an achievement becomes improbable due to misusing religious and spiritual formations in everyday societies. This is a pivotal point to highlight when discussing the participation of blacks in social progression.

Another point that should be highlighted when discussing the social trajectory of black people within the *New World* system of chattel enslavement is the degree to which elite Africans took part in the social ordeal, pitting uncoalesced hybrid blacks against coalesced hybrid blacks.

From the West African shoreline barracoons, fortified dungeons, canoes, and the hellish slave ship, and from the branding of black skin and selling thereof throughout the *New World*, newly coalesced hybrid blacks fought valiantly to regain their freedom. In contrast, uncoalesced hybrid blacks chose to submit, survive, and elevate themselves within the *New World* structure of oppression toward black skin. To be sure, all levels within the black sub-world experience the abuse of privilege, but it is the top tier of this experience that occupies more space and wields more power and influence over the lower-tier hybrid blacks. Such an imbalance of power deserves serious attention. This duality of the black lived experience can be traced from the moment elite Africans captured and sold less privileged and, at times, highly privileged Africans. Moreover, some privileged enslaved blacks became *watchdogs* over other enslaved blacks. As time progressed, newly freed blacks developed a disdain or lack of awareness about the black-skin trajectory in history.

COALESCED HYBRID BLACKS/ UNCOALESCED HYBRID BLACKS

I often ponder, if the problem of black skin is so grave, one would be well within reason to assume that the most enlightened blacks, scholars, for instance, would gladly descend from the ivory tower of affluence and prestige and sit among, in Howard Thurman's language, *the disinherited*.[6] Black scholarship that is not nuanced and issued to the black masses is merely an exercise of futility and elitism and is disconnected from any notion of social responsibility designed to make the black lived experience better for future generations. There are two distinct groups of consideration here. In the first group, the black intellectual refutes any racial categorization

6. See Thurman, *Jesus and the Disinherited*.

associated with the social experience of black skin. In the second group, one will discover black intellectuals who are so caught up within the inner workings of the *politics of corporate academy* that scholarship is merely expressed through peer review publications and culturally manicured spaces of engagement; for instance, campus programming, conferences, debates, societies, lectures, and so on.

In *Caste: The Origins of Our Discontent,* Isabel Wilkerson recollects hearing a lecture in London by a Nigerian-born playwright who forthrightly declared, "There are no black people in Africa. Africans are not black. They are Igbo and Yoruba, Ewe, Akan, Ndebele. They are not black. They are just themselves. They are humans on the land. That is how they see themselves, and that is who we are. They do not become black until they go to America or the U.K. It is then that they become black."[7] It seems to me that the thrust of this pronouncement is centered on notions of how Africans come to terms with self. As opposed to viewing self through a lens that negates a multifaceted African perspective, Africans, according to the former logic, understand themselves to be humans primarily with a distinction in tribal affiliation. Thus, the cultural distinction of European ways of understanding blackness does not trump, nor apply to, traditional or contemporary African value systems and ethics. I can certainly appreciate the spirit of the argument. Africans are distinct peoples with many cultural alignments and departures within the long trajectory of human history.

But Frantz Fanon reminds us that the enslavement of the Africans ushered in a new way of being human, a culturally hybrid black race.[8] In a very true sense, slavery codified the African experience. It birthed a new humanity that requires a new perspective in understanding the black/African mind, body, and soul and how the world responds to such a creation. The rejection of colonialism requires more than an intellectual refusal to align with projected images of racial categorizations, for instance, holding dearly to the notion that racism is not real. It is merely a social structure. Such refusals are necessary, but Fanon challenges the colonized and the colonizer to think more deeply about the psychological effect of colonialism's experience and practice and their effect on the human ability to overcome inherent oppression.[9] Moreover, refusing or denying a phenomenon, such

---

7. Wilkerson, *Caste,* 52–53.

8. Lewis Gordon would describe such a lived experience as the birth of anti-blackness. See Gordon, "Black and the Body Politic."

9. See Bernasconi, "Casting the Slough."

as enslavement, does not alleviate the cultural impact and influence that a phenomenon exerts upon humans on both conscious and unconscious levels. Blackness, as it were, is a cultural adaptation in which oppressed Africans became a unified group to form a new identity within a *New World*,[10] which required a new and collective way of promoting the themes of African-centered notions of survival and resistance.

Even if Ahmaud Arbery, for instance, refused to be confined to notions of blackness as they relate to the historical nature of systemic racism,[11] nevertheless, through cultural education on both conscious and unconscious levels, he becomes a victim of lynching simply because his skin is black. Even if Ahmaud, again, simply for argument's sake, had a history of denying the cultural implications of his black skin, such a denial would not have influenced the world around him. Greg McMichael, Travis McMichael, and Roddie Bryan viewed Ahmaud's black skin as a social negation of *other* and thus tried to forcefully question his presence in occupied white space. And because he refused to consent to such a cultural proscription, he was hunted, trapped, and systematically executed. Juxtapose Ahmaud's experience with black skin to that of other blacks who presume notions of systemic black oppression as passé, and one is left attempting to fill a proverbial gap of bewilderment, frustration, and a sense of cultural abandonment and, ultimately, pity.

I once talked with a black professor about writing, teaching, and other academic elements aligned with being a *scholar*. My colleague asserted that "publishing in newspapers is not authentic scholarship." I was tempted to present a rebuttal, but I took note of the comment and continued the conversation. The comment provided, however, tangible evidence to support the counter assertion that some black intellectual spaces, as erudite and

---

10. Nikole Hannah-Jones's *The 1619 Project: A New Origin Story* provides a good context for better understanding the racial dynamic in North America; however, Jones's analysis is limited in terms of understanding fully specific historical pivots across the *New World*, which, by 1619 and over two centuries, had developed specific cultural patterns that would come to influence both enslaved blacks and slave-holding whites.

11. If a pro-black reconstruction happened for black people after a bloody civil war, if parties could come to terms, the victor would have a position of leverage to have an attempt at the lion's share of the spoils, but because a civil war, although bloody and murderous, is fought between son and brother, uncle and cousin, there is a willingness to compromise in the interest of mending the physical, psychological, and economic dimensions of both North and South. If slavery was to be done away with, a proviso was presented as an occasional loophole to fill the coffers and reestablish the opportunities of the plantation owners.

pompous as they may present, lack the required cosmic conscious intelligence (i.e., the divine spark within) to deal effectively with the problem of black skin, and this is a travesty.

Considered the dean emeritus of black scholarship and intellectualism, W. E. B. Du Bois would also disagree with my colleague's conclusion based on his analysis of the problem of black skin. One should understand that good scholarship must be produced in various forms and at high rates to support a continuum of social engagement and cultural advancement, especially when confronting the problem of black skin. If white oppression is as bad as many believe it is, black scholars, it seems to me, should be on the front lines of this battle. Is not the saying "knowledge equates to power" the battle cry of the intelligentsia? As Harold Cruse notes in *The Crisis of the Black Intellectual*, the black intellectual "should tell black America how and why Negroes are trapped in this cultural degeneracy, and how it has dehumanized their essential identity, squeezed the lifeblood of their inherited cultural ingredients out of them, and then relegated them to the cultural slums."[12] Such persons could act as intelligence officers, sifting through records and postulating innovative ideas and theories on the black experience, whatever the field of study. That is, if racism is as bad as many say that it is. Every conceivable space for helping black-skinned people think more deeply about their plight in life should be investigated.[13]

Du Bois started this socially responsible pattern of intellectualism by producing transferable artifacts such as monographs, articles, essays, short stories, poems, prayers, novels, pamphlets, a visualization data book of the *color line*, and a publication for children explaining the events of the world surrounding their young black skin. During the 1970s, black scholars continued the fight that DuBois had begun with his 1899 publication *The Philadelphia Negro* and the 1903 publication *The Souls of Black Folk*. These scholars systematically published academic works on slave history, African philosophy and spirituality, and culture from a coalesced hybrid black-skin perspective while also presenting this academic research in media venues such as local community talks, newspapers, pamphlets, magazines,

---

12. Cruse, *Crisis*, 455.

13. In 1969, Kenneth Clark convened a meeting of prominent black intellectuals at Haverford College in Pennsylvania. The three-day conversation was focused on defining who they were as black people wanting to fully integrate into American society. Participants included Manie Phipps Clark, St. Clair Drake, Ralph Ellison, John Hope Franklin, William H. Hastie, Adelaide L. Hill, M. Carl Holman, Saunders Redding, Phyllis A. Wallace, and Robert C. Weaver. See Lackey, *Haverford Discussions*.

bulletins, periodicals, and talk shows. Because of these efforts, common black folk were more likely to mature consciously by learning historical truths related to the trek of the black lived experience.

Uncoalesced hybrid black scholars who choose *ivory tower* affiliation solely over mass movement interest and culturally correct education, often, even with the accomplishment of tenure, find themselves isolated in the proverbial corner on the bottom level of the corporate *ivory tower*. Because it, too, is tethered tightly to the American milieu of embedded racism. But they live, breathe, and gather meaning nonetheless by being strategically tethered to more white space than most blacks. It is interesting to note that Dr. King had several opportunities to attempt to hide from the experience of black-skin affiliation by accepting a deanship or professorship at several prominent institutions; thus, thriving in a quasi-safe corner bubble within the corporate *ivory tower*, but because he began to understand the problem of black skin to be tethered to a long memory of hatred, abuse, and miseducation, he decided to become a pastor, then a civil rights leader, while using his scholarly acumen still, to play an intricate part in reverting black-skin affiliation from a negative to a positive experience via his understanding of cosmic love and the divine spark within.

I have grappled with the problem of black skin since the tender age of ten, and I have discovered that significant factors such as generational trauma, the abuse of black privilege, educational practices, and outright white mob violence are often negated when addressing the matter of black oppression. The problem of black skin is frequently refuted with the assurance that life was vastly different one hundred or two hundred years ago. Moreover, because of educational opportunities and technological advancement of modern societies, suggesting that black skin presents a problem is an absurd and antiquated notion and should be done away with. Within some black spaces, such a refutation is endorsed and used as a measuring rod of success: *I made it, and so can you.* To this, I reply: time and chance separate me from an Ahmaud Arbery; time and chance. Regardless of the extent of social pedigree, no person with black skin is wholeheartedly safe and liberated in a world undergirded with racist ideology. No person with black skin is free until all people with black skin are free.

1

A MYTH OF BLACKNESS
(We Come from the Stars)

IN ANCIENT TIMES, PEOPLES of the world crafted stories about how the universe was formed and came into existence. These crafted stories also explained how supernatural beings took part in this development and how these same beings began constructing humanity. Traditional stories, also known as myths, are sometimes interpreted as being *make-believe* and/or full of exaggeration; to be fair, I understand why this could be the case based on the purposeful ways in which people are formally and informally educated. However, one would be wise to avoid such a biased misunderstanding when dealing with ancient myths, especially regarding the myth of blackness.

I.

Traditionally, myths are merely ways in which history is recorded and shared throughout generations in written and oral forms. Wherever ancient peoples were situated geographically, something innate suggested that the group in which they found themselves was distinct from any other group, and such a distinction also entailed origin stories that provided a sense of meaning and purpose for their daily lives. To help unravel this mystery of cosmic creation in modern times, the late scholar Sylvia Wynter used the term *Homo Narran* when describing the anatomically related species of humanity and the desire to define cultural meaning via storytelling. First, according to Wynter, early humans began the process of cultural meaning by unraveling the universe's origin. This process entails investigating the so-called cosmic explosion, what we today would refer to as the big bang.[1] The big bang offers a conceptual way to better understand the significance of oneness while embracing its complexities and cosmic variations.

The Mesopotamian origin story, the Enuma Elish,[2] for instance, relates how order comes into existence because of a battle in the cosmos between Goddess Tiamat, the primordial energy and mother of the race of gods, and Marduk, the god of wisdom with four eyes and four ears. As the story goes, Marduk kills Tiamat in battle and creates the first human being with the purpose and duty to serve the gods. Ancient peoples of the Americas also have unique creation myths. The Mayans, for instance, believe in Tepeu, known as the Maker, and Gucumatz, the feathered Spirit, and the Lakota tell of Inyan as the sole creator and all-sustaining force of the cosmos.

Across the Atlantic Ocean on the continent of Africa, the Mande people in southern Mali believe that the *Energetic Presence* caused several seeds to blow up; thus, animals and humans were created. With colorful illustrations, the Yoruba tell of the Sky People and the duties associated with Olorun and Orishas. The Dogon of Mali also speaks of a cosmic development by highlighting the engagement between Amma and Ogo, who stand for order and chaos. Even more interesting is what Professor Sylvester James Gates, a leading black theoretical physicist specializing in superstring theory and supersymmetry, thinks about ancient African Dogon/Akan symbols known as Adinkra codes. According to Gates, these geometric patterns create the math that balances the universe; in short, these Dogon/Akan error-correcting codes provide the cosmic context for which the universe has kept a certain equilibrium since the cosmic blast, which I find pretty remarkable.[3]

---

1. Sylvia Wynter relied upon Franz Fanon's paradigm of the origin of the human as a "hybrid-auto-instituting-languaging-storytelling species: bios/mythoi." See Wynter and McKittrick, "Unparalleled Catastrophe," 25.

2. See L. King, *Enuma Elish*.

3. It should be noted that it is reasonable to argue that the ancient peoples of the world were equally as destructive as their descendants, or even more so. And this is certainly a fair criticism. The Yamnaya people of Europe, for instance, as well as the Aztecs, the Zulu of South Africa under the leadership and military commander Shaka, and the Mongols under the leadership of Genghis Khan supply noteworthy evidence that the ancient world was undoubtedly barbaric. However, minor factions in the ancient world had forgotten or forbidden knowledge about the theme of universal oneness despite cultural variations and violent tendencies.

Regardless of the various degrees of difference, ancient peoples began recording the written and oral history of cultures beyond their contemporary generations. These enlightened humans pushed further back and began raising and answering questions that focused on the beginning of humanity, the purpose of nature, and the essence of the cosmos. Because of their point of departure, ancient cultures developed a deep awareness of the creator and their significant connection to the development of humanity. The world in which we live today rarely provides the intellectual spacing to appreciate the whole of a matter; instead, because of the lack of looking further back into the cosmic experience of humanity, people are systematically programmed to focus on the perceived negative parts, such as skin color. Humans, despite the difference in skin tone and cultural variability, have markers of genetic relation and, outside the scope of accidental trauma, defect, and genetic manipulation, present with standard anatomical features and functionality such as a nose, mouth, arms, and legs.

II.

It is mind-boggling that a particular group of human beings has been subject to social ridicule because of skin color. This fact is utterly absurd; nevertheless, it is an absurdity that has been a constant theme within the American social milieu for several centuries. Throughout the unraveling phases of these periods, whites would come to define blacks as being something *other* than human; similarly, blacks, in the act of psychological retaliation, would come to define whites as nonhuman based on their depravity and treatment of black skin. This cultural exchange is an element in the analysis of the problem of black skin that is readily overlooked, rejected, or ignored. In a sense, both black and white people remain trapped in a knowledge system that fails to acknowledge the stories of what it means to be human despite these noticeable variations of culture, specifically, origin stories that explain who and what we are in a narratively constructed manner, down to skin color.[4] For well over one hundred years, however, black writers and thinkers have produced elevated levels of research to connect the cultural dots of the black experience beyond that of chattel enslavement in the *New World* plantation systems of the Americas and Caribbean Islands. This effort, I imagine, was an attempt to remedy the dysfunctional thinking associated with having black skin. I think the most controversial matters that have

---

4. See Mignolo, "Sylvia Wynter."

been debated and researched are the notions that humanity was birthed out of Africa and that Africans' first encounter with the shores of the Americas was not situated in the experience of chattel enslavement.

There is consensus within a specific school of thought that the first black came out of Africa through the "Strait of Gibraltar, the Isthmus of Suez, and maybe through Sicily and Southern Italy" several thousand years ago, a migrating black known as the Grimaldi Man, also the first inhabitant of Europe.[5] This point of view reached its apex nearly twenty years ago. Over the past several years, recent archaeological and anthropological research does not contradict this perspective; it merely suggests that what we believed about cultural developments and migrations of blackness has been misunderstood regarding dates, particular artifacts, and when certain human and cultural advancements occurred. In other words, what we know as the migration of civilization through blackness did happen, but it happened further back than what normative research would allow us to consider. Especially the matter of ancient blacks in Mesoamerica.

Suppose one wishes to consider reading about the interactions and influences ancient blacks had on the cultural development of Mesoamerica. In that case, I recommend Ivan van Sertima's late-twentieth-century, highly debated classic, *They Came Before Columbus*. He argues that the Olmec, the first known civilization in Mesoamerica, began as a culture in 800 and faded into the hidden memory of history in 400 BCE. The crux of his research is to show that ancient Africans and Mesoamericans share similarities in tobacco use, trading practices, and physical attributes and that ancient Africans possessed the skill and technology to effectively maneuver beyond their location on land and water.[6]

Some readers of his research mistakenly conclude that Van Sertima is being arrogantly presumptuous to claim that the ancient Mesoamerican people were devoid of cultural ideals until an engagement with African ingenuity was experienced; moreover, detractors warn, Van Sertima's proposed correlation between the Olmec colossi heads and Nubian black facial features is problematic and ethnocentric in nature. The latter seems to be the biggest affront on the list of critiques. In 2020, Ann Cyphers and her colleagues at Universidad Nacional Autónoma de Mexico added to this list

---

5. Diop, *Civilization or Barbarism*, 11–13; Wells, *Journey*, 191. See Diop, *African Origin*.

6. Van Sertima, *They Came Before Columbus*, 148. I also recommend Diop, *African Origin* and *Civilization or Barbarism*.

by finding mitochondrial DNA in human remains discovered in Vera Cruz. Therefore, confirming that the originators of the Olmec heads are not African proves that the indigenous peoples of Mesoamerica were not African; instead, the studied DNA provided evidence that contemporary Mexicans in the same region have matching DNA.[7] This is commendable work, but I observe something unique in this situation that deserves highlighting. The current findings are indeed the current findings. However, this does not disprove an initial black presence in Mesoamerica.

The current evidence proves only that at the moment in time, certain people lived and died in a particular area and region. This cannot be refuted. The academic study of Mesoamerica colossal heads did not commence until 1939.[8] With carbon-dating technology implemented in archeological studies in 1946, we have yet to reach the one-hundred-year mark in analytical research of Mesoamerica.[9] Although colossal heads have been found in San Lorenzo (ten), La Venta (four), Tres Zapotes (two), and La Cobata (one), I suspect more ancient artifacts and reliefs will be found with more time and excavation because ancient Africa, known in ancient languages as *Gondwanaland*,[10] was connected with South America, India, and Australia 3 million years ago, and a Stone Age axe was discovered in northern Africa, dating back 1.3 million years.[11] I believe more million-year discoveries will provide evidence regarding the significance of blackness to Mesoamerican studies.

Additionally, noted linguist and anthropologist Clyde Winters[12] agrees that Van Sertima was presumptuous when asserting that ancient Nubians made first contact with the people of Mesoamerica. According to Winters, it was the Mande people rather than the Nubians who influenced the people of Mesoamerica, and this is proven via writing patterns between the North Africans and the early Olmecs that he has studied and deciphered as well as evidence of African skeletons at the Olmec sites of Monte Alban,

7. Lopez, "Olmec Colossal Heads."
8. Van Sertima, *They Came Before Columbus*, 145.
9. Van Sertima, *They Came Before Columbus*, 145.
10. Du Bois, *World and Africa*, 81–82. This landmass was divided due to the changes resulting from the rift valleys.
11. *Al Jazeera*, "Stone Age Axe."
12. Professor Winters is author of *African Empires in Ancient America*; *The Ancient Black Civilizations of Asia*; *Atlantis in Mexico*; *Ancient Scripts in South America*; *The Phylogeography of Afro Americans*; *We Are Not Just Africans: The Black Native Americans*; and *Archaeological Decipherment of Ancient Writing Systems*.

Cerro de las Mesas, and Tlatilco, which were discovered in the 1970s.[13] Current research places humans in what is now known as Mexico 12,000 to 15,000 years ago. Additionally, contemporary Mexicans mainly consist of indigenous Americans, Spanish immigrants, and the African enslaved.[14] At some juncture along the historical timeline, the Olmec, according to Van Sertima, became people of three faces. They were Asian, Black, and Mediterranean.

> These faces became one face, to which the broad name "Olmec" was given. I think it is necessary to make it clear—since partisan and ethnocentric scholarship seems to be the order of the day—that the emergence of the Negroid face, which the archaeological and cultural data overwhelmingly confirms, in no way presupposes that lack of a native originality, the absence of other influences, or the automatic eclipse of other faces. Fusion is the marriage—not the collision—of cultures.[15]

In the final analysis, Van Sertima merely outlines the neglected cultural potentialities of black influence on Mesoamerican culture. He adds to the long and complicated history of the constantly evolving peoples of the region. This history entails that in the south-central area of Mexico (i.e., Mesoamerica), civilizations such as the Olmecs, Aztecs, Maya, Teotihuacan, Toltec, and Zapotec civilizations thrived. However, things would change when these people came into contact with Europeans in the early 1500s. To Van Sertima's point, it is essential to not locate blacks to the region with just the experience of sixteenth-century slavery. Vera Cruz, a central location for importing African slaves, would become a space and cultural identification of black Mexicans for future generations. Out of this heritage, a black Indian named Vicente Guerrero would become Mexico's first president in 1829 and, with such power, free the African enslaved.[16] Thus making Mexico a staple of black cultural influence.

---

13. See Winters, "Nubians and Olmecs."
14. Bodner et al., "Mitochondrial DNA," s.v. "Introduction."
15. Van Sertima, *They Came Before Columbus*, 149.
16. Katz, *Black Indians*, 51.

III.

At least at some juncture along the several cycles on the historical timeline, humanity was born through blackness and went ahead to stretch forth and populate the world by modifying various skin tones, textures, and communication. Blackness, as it is understood today, is more ancient than the leading evidence suggests, which finds people with black skin on the shores of Africa or even the early Americas, Middle East, or Asia. In the spirit of Wynter, one must push a bit further and begin the investigation outside of traditional ways of thinking about history, religion, archaeology, and anthropology to grasp the fullness of blackness. One must investigate the physics associated with the so-called big bang and cosmic blackness.

Before, there was substance in which to form humanity, which would eventually morph into the phenomenon we know as black skin; there was a proceeding event, a cosmic big bang. The invisible made things visible at some juncture outside our limited understanding of physics. It was a thought, or better yet, a Word, that got the proverbial cosmic ball rolling. The ancient word *AUM* or *Om* of African and Sanskrit origins declares this sound to be the foundational thread linking us to better understanding the processes of that precise moment the realities of the seen cosmos became an extension of its unseen Creator. John the apostle would argue that the Greek logos, *the Word*, the essence of divine creation, commanded everything in the cosmos to form. Moreover, the *Word* is a particular *Power* that uses sound and vibrations to manifest a tangible existence.

The big bang was an intricate process of *Power* in which humanity, Earth, and the known and unknown cosmos harnessed energy to replicate the divine essence of the Creator. I am unsure if there were multiple big bangs, nor am I sure, like Chanda Prescod-Weinstein, that there was just one,[17] but the world (i.e., the universe) I reflect on is said to be 13.8 billion years old. By articulating a Word or formulating a thought articulating a *Word*, the universe expanded in a burst and looked the same in every conceivable direction. Prescod-Weinstein refers to such a movement as a process of *sameness*; then, as it happens, it is likely at some point of this *sameness* that particles formed both matter and antimatter, but more matter.[18] Stars eventually came into existence and illuminated time and space through, possibly, the myriad of cosmic explosions, which presented in a

---

17. See Prescod-Weinstein, *Disordered Cosmos*, 68.
18. Prescod-Weinstein, *Disordered Cosmos*, 1–8.

new form as supernovae; thus, carbon and oxygen were born and would provide a process of life on planet Earth. As time-space expanded, due to cultural diversity and meaning-making initiatives, humans began creating myths and stories with cultural significance and meaning that aid in educating how a particular group of humans came to exist out of this cosmic explosion of *cosmic conscious intelligence*.[19]

IV.

On December 25, 2021, the James Webb Space Telescope (JWST) was launched into space with the privilege of being the most advanced telescope ever built to investigate the first galaxies and other tangible phenomena that came forth from the cosmic explosion. Over the next several years, the telescope should continue to capture amazing photos of divine cosmic poetry in motion.[20] Even more fascinating is that, according to some physicists, 27 percent of the universe is dark matter, and 68 percent of the universe is what cosmologist Michael Turner calls dark energy.[21] Thus, 95 percent of the energetic forces around humans go unnoticed, unappreciated, and unused. In a correlative fashion, humans currently use only 2 percent of DNA protein capacity. The other 98 percent is called junk by leading scientists and researchers.[22] But this unused part of humanity is far more than just proverbial junk. It is there for a reason, even if we do not fully understand its potential. Also noteworthy is that, according to Michio Kaku, there are one hundred billion stars in our Milky Way galaxy; interestingly enough, we have the same number of neurons in the human brain.[23] Based on these correlations, it seems as if certain parts of the human body mirror the mode and function of the cosmos, which makes me think more intently about Professor Gates's theory regarding the probability that what we know as life

---

19. Selbie, *Physics of God*, 40, 139.

20. Once humans discover the nuances associated with the beginning of the big bang, I wonder what will be found beyond such an experience. Can anything be beyond the beyond? My contention is yes. I hold the belief that *I don't know until I know*. What if the point at the beyond is simply void of existence? I also believe that we exist in a multiverse schema, which means there are many more similar universes in the cosmos. Considering our universe alone has billions of galaxies, the reality of existing in a cosmic space of various potentialities is appealing and culturally promising.

21. Clegg, *Dark Matter*, 1, 10–11.

22. Clegg, *Dark Matter*, 1, 10–11.

23. Kaku, *Future of the Mind*, 1.

is merely a sophisticated coding system. This begs the question: What if humans, not simply a select few but all of humanity, were taught at a formative age the exhaustive potential behind the coding process of the origin of the cosmos? Moreover, what if humans, by chance, were educated in such a way to harness the ability to tap into junk DNA and begin the process of healing ailments outside of commercial pharmaceutical aid? I suspect our world would be a more functional place of human progression and equality.

Although the James Webb telescope is considered cutting edge and the latest technology for observing our universe and the cosmos as a whole, the late Zulu traditional healer, shaman, and cosmic historian Credo Mutwa taught that ancient beings from the Sirius B star system first visited the Dogon and the Zulu peoples of Africa several thousand years ago and taught them the structure and meaning of the cosmos.[24] The Dogon knew not only about Sirius A but also had intricate descriptions of Sirius B and C despite them being too small to see with human eyes. Robert Temple's famed work *The Sirius Mystery: New Scientific Evidence of Alien Contact 5,000 Years Ago* and Marcel Griaule and Germaine Dieterlen's *The Pale Fox* further substantiate the claim that the Dogon were aware of advanced beings and cosmological technologies before many so-called experts commenced the process of researching the Sirius constellation, and that the Dogon know of four other invisible *heavenly bodies* in the Sirius system.[25] It cannot be overstated that the Sirius constellation plays a significant part in the story of blackness. One would be inclined to dismiss such significance due to unfamiliarity with the story and a carefully honed bias toward information that runs counter and, in some cases, presents absurd contradictions to the orthodox teaching of biblical history. Therefore, I would like to prepare the reader with a thought that could assist in dismantling such thinking.

As a religious studies graduate student, I sought a balanced education by studying in consecutive, liberal, and radical academic spaces. After experiencing exceptional instruction in fields such as New Testament, Hebrew, and Old Testament studies, I presumed I would be ready to become a professor when the time arose. I was not. When teaching a class in ethics, I would often struggle to effectively challenge students to think critically about the Joshua narrative and consider the ethical reasoning behind a man

---

24. The Zulu also have a myth associated with coming from Mars to Earth after a galactic war left Mars uninhabitable. During the 1970s, we discovered that there were pyramids on Mars. See Ashby, *Egyptian Yoga*, 1:65.

25. Temple, *Sirius Mystery*, 71.

who professed to receive secondhand information from Moses about God's desire for him to commit genocide. To be sure, such behavior was considered permissible because the Hebrews could use more space.[26] In a sense, I wanted my students to pivot from the typical sermon, Sunday school format, and vacation Bible school teachings and give agency to the people of the so-called occupied lands. The ethical point of consideration was that these often-marginalized peoples, including the Amorites, the Girgashites, the Hittites, the Hivites, the Jebusites, and the Perizzites, because of a narrow frame of instructional reference, were viewed as *other* and later denied the essence of human personality and worth.

I tried to teach students that these people of Canaan had relationships, cultural inheritance, daily obligations, and feelings associated with being human, such as love, hope, aspirations, and divine substance. However, these ethical considerations are often absent when Joshua's narrative is preached and reflected upon. It was primarily black students who had the most difficulty with this intellectual exercise in moral reasoning. Many failed to see themselves as cultural correlations to the narrative of privilege, power, and social manipulation. They did not see that these vanquished peoples of the land were their cultural cousins and that they were also victims of the practice of manifest destiny. To this end, I caution the reader to, as much as possible, set aside biases about *unequivocally* knowing what is considered closed canonization of the biblical text and its cultural privileging. Instead, for the sake of ethical consideration, one must ponder if cultural understanding is limited, even if one has traversed the hallowed halls of the academy for several years; one must ponder still what if understanding is limited to the ability of a carefully orchestrated discipline of study. And for the novice who has been a proverbial sponge for information under such instruction, the task is the same.

V.

The following thought I present is beyond the norm of traditional reading and instruction. This, I must admit. To the uninitiated, it may be read as taboo, peculiar, and, to a more significant extent, unacceptable and counter to respected scholastic endeavors. But I must again caution readers, particularly black readers, to hold firm to the intellectual rod of balance. Reject the

---

26. Another ethical point of consideration that deepens such an analysis is the presence of Black Jews in Africa and the Americas. See Parfitt's *Black Jews*.

trained subconscious's reaction of self-denial and hold fast to the ancient African adage *know thyself*. The task, as has been the traditional trajectory of the authentic black intellectual for many generations, is to bring to conscious awareness those words of meaning that could potentially unlock the dormant spirit of heritage and significance deep within the black soul.

As I alluded to, there is something unique about the Dogon and their advanced technological understanding of ancient cosmic arrangements, which remained hidden from the most advanced human technology for thousands of years. Dogon history is a fascinating tale in which they credit the founding of their civilization to an amphibious race from the Sirius B star system, which they call the *Nommo(s)*. It is a Dogon traditional belief that the Nommo, also known as *Masters of the Water*, the *Instructors*, or *Monitors*, traveled to Earth in a spacecraft that resembled an ark vehicle, which also had rotating functionalities. The Dogon teach that this encounter with star beings happened deep within their cultural past near the regions of Egypt and the Middle East, rather than their emigrational point of locale in Mali. The Dogon also noted two spacecraft in view upon this first visitation. A mother ship hovered in the sky at a distance, which they call *ie pelu tolo* (i.e., star of the tenth moon), and the rocket craft that landed. Temple notes that this mother ship, which the Nommo revere as a star, cannot be seen until the mother ship prepares to descend back to Earth, which they promised the Dogon they would do. He also suggests that the star of the tenth moon is Saturn's tenth main moon, Phoebe.[27] Upon such a return, the unseen star will appear in the sky, and the aquatic beings will commence with what they call *the Day of the Fish*.

Interestingly, other cultural groups display remarkable similarities to Dogon's myth of creation by fishlike beings, creators of the water. For instance, the Chinese have a myth about their founding by an amphibious being (i.e., a being with a man's head and a fish tail) named Fuxi.[28] But the ones that intersect with the myth of the Dogon in the location of ancient blackness are the Mesopotamian (i.e., Sumer, Akkad, Babylonia, and Assyria) myths of creation.

If one is not careful here, it is likely to consciously or unconsciously presume that Mesopotamia, although not completely white, is not actually black skinned either. This is because of how someone views or places their understanding of blackness at a particular place and time. I wish to

27. Temple, *Sirius Mystery*, 295–99.
28. Temple, *Sirius Mystery*, 289.

highlight a time in history, prehistory, that shows a trajectory of what we know as the partial point of the origin of blackness. It begins with the belief that modern humans have been on this planet for at least 2 million years. We have a common ancestor with the hominin species *Homo erectus*. The early human ancestor migrated east out of Africa into what we now call Iraq with nimble fingers, a large brain, and developed legs for walking; additionally, early ancestors occupied the lands of Asia, down the East African coast, in Kenya, Tanzania, Mozambique, up and across northeast Africa from Sudan, Egypt, Libya, and Morocco. Our most recent ancestor, the *Homo sapiens*, 200,000 years ago migrated to Morocco and across the top of the north continent, east, and down to South Africa. It is believed that we lived and bred with other hominins called *Homo neanderthalensis*, *Homo floresiensis*, and *Denisovans*.[29]

The first people we know of to record the history of their interaction between themselves and the world, and above them in Mesopotamia, were called *Sumerian Blackheads*.[30] In fact, as Charles B. Copher noted in the late twentieth century, the black presence in the Bible originates in Mesopotamia under the leadership of the black warrior/king Nimrod, son of Cush.[31] Moreover, ancient black Mesopotamian myths are essential points of attention because the writings of those cultures, such as Sumer, Akkad, Babylonia, and Assyria, predate the more well-known and accepted biblical writings. For instance, the biblical account of the flood is copied from early writings such as the Epic of Gilgamesh, the book of Enoch, and Atra-Hasis. Additionally, the biblical story of Eden uses language that one would see in earlier Akkadian and Sumerian versions of the stories.[32]

VI.

In this new land, the ancient, ancient black people of Mesopotamia chronicled a myth of a fishlike god named Ea, or Enki, in Sumerian and Babylonian

---

29. The first hominin on the continent of Africa was 7 million years ago. It is posited that hominin was a smaller canine ancestor called *Sahelanthropus tchadensis*, found in modern-day Chad. See American Museum of Natural History, "Anne and Bernard Spitzer Hall."

30. McCray, *Black Presence*, 1:90–91.

31. Copher, "Black Presence."

32. Adamo, *Africa*, notes that the Myth of Adapa, the Epic of Gilgamesh, and the Enki Ninhursag Paradise narrative go also with what is said about the versions being dated earlier than the biblical one.

THE PROBLEM OF BLACK SKIN

tales, a god of water who sleeps in a freshwater receptacle called the Abzu.[33] Enki is associated with the Mesopotamian royal trinity in the story, including his father, who rules from above, Anu; and his brother, the god of Earth, Enlil.[34] He also has a sister named Ninhasak, in Egyptian myth known as Isis, who would take early primate eggs through genetic manipulation, give birth to Adam, and produce Eve through DNA cloning.[35] Enlil also plays an essential role in the life pattern of black people on planet Earth. He should be considered the first to set before black people a program of divide and conquer, and for the most part, he has been successful.[36] Also, according to the ancient Babylonian text the Enuma Elish, better known as the Seven Tablets of Creation, the Sirian Anunnaki were albino, black, red, and blue skinned with West African traits. They are diverse people. Due to climate issues, Nibiru, their Anunnaki Sirian planet of habitation, looked to remedy this clear and present danger using technology, which required a precise metal to resist radiation. So, Sirian Anunnaki came to earth 450,000 years ago to mine gold and contact our hominin cousins.[37]

The term "Anunnaki"[38] (i.e., those from above) is connected to the ancient myth of King Anu.[39] These Anunnaki were galactic refugees from many alien species, presenting with many shades and human and feline characteristics.[40] They landed in the Mesopotamian region of modern-day Iraq.[41] According to Sumerian texts, Amun-Ra is an immortal Anunnaki

---

33. Adamo, *Africa*, 32.

34. Also known as the biblical Yahweh of the Old Testament, Enlil became quite agitated when he learned that the diverse human population had used a common language to reach the heights of heaven. So, he confused their language and scattered them across the land and gave them markers according to the Anunnaki that looked like them.

35. See Wagner and Briggs, *Penultimate Curiosity*, 351–56.

36. Genesis 11 states the modified life span for humans would be 120 years. See also Poszewiecka et al., "Revised Time." In addition to this, Enlil placed telomere caps on the ends of the human chromosomes and reduced human life to the maximum of 120 years.

37. See Num 13:13, 22, 28; Deut 1:28; 2:10–11, 21; 9:2; Josh 11:21–22; 14:12; Judg 1:20.

38. Brisch, "Anunna."

39. Hopper, "Anu-Father of the Gods."

40. Sigdell, *Reign of the Anunnaki*, vii, 9, 11–21, 1067; Kasten, *Alien World Order*, 118–19.

41. The late historian of religions scholar Charles Long would refer to such a cultural contact as evidence of a cargo cult experience in which an imbalance of power is present. For instance, whatever myths these early Indigenous hominins conceptualized about their worth and connection to a higher source of energy were replaced by the presence of beings that were far more advanced than their primitive minds could intelligently

known as Marduk, the chief Babylonian god. Surprisingly enough, Marduk is also the son of Enki. The ancient Anunnaki that came to Earth, in some intricate manner of social engagement, created a new cultural context for black skin. Considering this historical timeline, I believe having black skin associated with a cosmic past full of meaning and significance cross-culturally is most beneficial. Especially when it is a story about the enslaved African ancestors, whom blacks venerate as being both wise and guiding, who harnessed themselves to the psychic powers of their ancient ancestors and held on to know that the *Day of the Fish* was coming.

Because of the socialization effect chattel enslavement had on blacks, the *Day of the Fish* has been exchanged for the *Day of the Lord,* a Christian reference to awaiting the coming of Christ, who would handle releasing blacks from the yoke of oppression. Another consideration entails pivoting from slave religion to a more focused Christianized mode of worship and faith system. Labeled as pagan and harmful, slave religion used African spirituality and practices to constantly remind the enslaved of their heritage of ancestral greatness. As the solid African body, mind, and spirit had nearly succumbed to the ravenous applications of *New World* chattel enslavement, I can hear the enslaved priest and priestess of *ole* move ever so gently betwixt and between their befuddled chained brothers and sisters in arms, drenched with blood, sweat, and tears, the religious leaders communicate with the downtrodden with eyes of both empathy and resolve, *hold fast, we come from the stars.*

---

process; thus, with ease, the old myth of unseen cosmic significance was simply replaced with the newly constructed myth of seen cosmic importance in meeting the Anunnaki in the flesh. See Long, *Significations*, 127–29; Du Bois, *World and Africa*, 119.

2

IGNORANCE, ARROGANCE, AND THE *THING*

It still astonishes me how, the more work one does, the more difficult it becomes, the more impossible the task.[1]

—Toni Morrison

HUMANS HAVE THE TENDENCY to become siloed in ways of thinking about and through notions of oppression, particularly concerning the problem of blackness in America and the surrounding corners of the globe. What humans consider deep analytical work on race becomes flawed due to individual experiences, education, and social associations, which assist in undergirding motivations for how reality should be lived, digested, and interpreted. Even those who hold the noblest of intentions in explaining race dynamics often do so with a limited understanding of the essence of black oppression and what W. E. B. Du Bois would refer to as the *Thing*, the ever-elusive truth and crux of a matter. To be sure, I bring a level of ignorance and arrogance to this critical essay. I know there are multiple layers to unearth before one arrives at a coherent resolution of the *Thing*. But getting at the crux of racial oppression, as tedious as it may present, is certainly achievable. Scholars and intellectuals have pushed beyond ignorance and

---

1. T. Morrison, *Source*, 247.

IGNORANCE, ARROGANCE, AND THE *THING*

arrogance to finally confront the *Thing*, only to discover that they lacked a strong and intellectually honest populace to help strategically address *It*.

I.

No doubt literature is written, classes are taught, campaigns announced, debates had, media platforms established, and monies endowed; still, the *Thing* remains elusive, not solely because of its insidious nature, but rather, because both ignorance and arrogance play functional roles in alerting people who do work in the area of race analysis that their notion of the matter is the most viable based on their lived experience of education, personal associations, and understanding of the world around them. I find my first acknowledged moment of ignorance and arrogance about race analysis as a bright-eyed young man who is prepared (or certainly believes this to be the case) to engage freedom and the world around me.

Several weeks after my high school graduation, a momentous occasion for many a young person, I recall hearing news of the killing of a man in Jasper, Texas, James Byrd Jr., a black human being who was beaten, had chains wrapped around his ankles, then was dragged for three miles at an accelerated speed until his head and right arm, while conscious still, were severed from his body. The white men who committed this infamous crime, two of whom were subsequently executed, and one, Shawn Berry, who received life with eligibility for parole in 2038, no doubt believed that they were doing a just deed based on notions of black *otherness* and the role of whiteness as a distributor of arbitrary justice, correcting the balance of the world around them. James Byrd was killed because he looked a certain way. He had black skin—a marker of social resentment, and this factor is the limit of the analytical skills of the three cowardly murderers.

Being present in the moment of this lived experience, my cultural awareness should have been elevated, but to my chagrin, it was not. I am tempted to argue that this lack of cultural understanding is merely an example of the human maturation process. I was a young man with other thoughts and concerns; for instance, being preoccupied with transitioning into college the following fall was one distraction that I presume clouded my mental faculties. I recall viewing media segments on the murder. I even recall family members acknowledging that what happened to James Byrd Jr. was wrong and evil. Still, it was evil that had been happening to black people, confirmed and unconfirmed, for centuries in America. I was cautioned to be careful. But what does *being careful* mean in a racially charged social structure? How might I maneuver in a way that may prevent what happened to James Byrd Jr. from happening to me?

At that moment, I learned extraordinarily little from the experience of James Byrd's death. I do not recall giving the tragic event much thought beyond that *summer of inflection.* Nor do I remember being intrigued by conversations about protests or being privy to any clandestine discussions about the nature and future of the black race in America. This reflection is not to suggest that black people were not engaged in conversation and protest; instead, I suggest that conversation and protest were not at a level that would claim the attention of an ignorant and arrogant black teenager who was merely focused on the future of the inner world of self. At that level of limited social analysis and awareness, however, I did have strong feelings about what happened to Mr. Byrd. I had a visceral sense of awe and sadness. Still, I also reasoned *that it was terrible. Don't let it happen to you. Enjoy your life.* More than twenty years would pass before I would be able to give critical thought and understand the social implications of the lynching of James Byrd Jr.

On May 25, 2020, George Floyd Jr. experienced a horrific death as former Minneapolis police officer Derek Chauvin strangled him on the ground with his knee while Floyd was handcuffed and submissive for nine minutes and twenty-nine seconds.[2] I am no longer a naive young man with a significant degree of ignorance governing how I view myself and the world around me. I presumed to be better prepared to interpret the moment's significance. My thinking arises from my experience as a professor and in publishing work at the intersection of race, religion, culture, and society; despite the former, I was escorted merely from a low level of ignorance to an advanced level of arrogance. After years of academic work and navigating social terrain on the periphery of blackness, I now presumed that I possessed the ability to describe that moment of George Floyd Jr.'s murder as being tethered to a long history of oppression that also claimed

---

2. When the final observation and analysis of Emmett Till's body was completed, it looked like someone had taken a knife through him. His right eye was almost gone. The entire back of his head was knocked off. A neighbor nearby, who was a little boy himself, heard Emmett crying out to God—begging these cowards to stop; and like George Floyd Jr. he called out for his mother. When all was said and done, Till suffered a fractured thigh bone. Both wrists were broken. Part of one ear was missing. Barbed wire/heavy gin was placed around his neck, and he was thrown in the Tallahatchie River. See Hudson-Weems, *Emmett Till.*

the life of James Byrd Jr. and so many others; by doing so, I envisioned a type of unification of blackness that would reemerge in the spirit of the ancestors from many moons ago. I had this thought because of historical pivots I saw potentially shifting America's cultural and social landscape. For the first time in recorded history, for instance, every notable locale on the globe responded to the murder of a black person, George Floyd Jr., with marches and protests.

I was most impressed seeing young black and white children marching together, chanting, "Black lives matter." I envisioned a future of hope, a future that Louis Armstrong uttered optimistically years ago in "What a Wonderful World." But then I decided to press deeper into the matter and understood that an element of contextual psychosis is associated with such a thought. What Louis Armstrong describes is certainly achievable, but considering the chaotic history of oppression, greed, savagery, and manipulation throughout world history, such an ambition would require tremendous energy and effort to remedy it fully. This is not to suggest that generational growth is undesirable. I believe this to be a worthy ambition, but I do not think that generational growth has occurred to the point of making meaningful change as it relates to the *black zeitgeist* addressing the *Thing*.

II.

It must be noted that although self-actualized, the *black zeitgeist* (i.e., the Spirit of Black Progression) grows in power only when energized with wisdom and knowledge around notions of objective truth. By increasing power within one person, the *black zeitgeist* can influence many others with passion, knowledge, courage, and understanding. This is how movements are born and expanded. One spark can set a home ablaze. If not held, flames desire to jump and connect with other flames to concentrate energy and grow, potentially consuming everything within their influence. This power can govern movements, but it seems to me that the black spirit is willing, but the flesh is weak. The spirit needs to feed on unmitigated truth, and this reality has been an element that the current social order keeps a muzzle on, as it were. The black spirit stands ready to defend righteousness and fight for social liberation. Denying enslaved blacks the truth about their culture and the world around them afforded an adapted black psyche to be set up;

thus, some blacks acquiesced to the notion of black inferiority, but many others did not.

So, the *black zeitgeist* pressed on at a high vibrational level until 1968, when Dr. King was assassinated. After this, the lack of high vibrational leadership produced generations that focused on creating more economic opportunity, legally and illegally, for black Americans and less on fighting to change a system designed to marginalize black social and financial aspirations. This low level of energy concerning black social engagement and cultural amnesia is seen in the lack of mobilization against the contemporary push to keep social dominance over black people by limiting the knowledge of what occurred in the historical trek of black life in America and the world. For instance, several state governments have enacted legislation that will intentionally circumvent efforts to forge a discussion about the historical progression behind the cultural experience between black and white people in America. Moreover, it is reasonable to conclude that many children are not growing into intellectually honest adults. All education requires a sense of direction; the question must be raised: Where are we taking them, and where has the knowledge taken us?

Unfortunately, children in America, many of whom will one day likely become adults with power and control, are guided down a path of intellectual distractions. I also think that Armstrong's vision of hope will soon morph into an experience of despair. If those black and white children fall victim to the standard educational system of control that America presents as superb, rather than reject it, their hearts could consciously and unconsciously see one another via frames of ignorance and arrogance. If not addressed fully, ignorance and arrogance present only a reiteration of ethics, values, and social understandings handed down via religion, education, law, media, and so on. To become a successful investment venture, *New World* slavery required the consent of society through its law, religion, and education.[3] This sobering reality lures me into thinking about the inherent pureness of children; yes, it also forces me to acknowledge that social structures make the probability of prolonged struggle together, as it currently stands, untenable.

As social beings, children are thrust into human networks and groups that help provide an awareness of what it means to exist as they are. Social mores educate people on how to think and behave in particular ways, proving they are part of the group. This is shown even in a biracial dynamic; for

---

3. See Young, *Rituals of Resistance*, 13.

instance, during Supreme Court Justice Amy Coney Barrett's confirmation hearing in 2020, Barrett was unable to name a recent book or any peer-reviewed studies that discuss racial disparities and inequities for black people in America. Senator Cory Booker pressed her on this matter and asserted that he was, in a sense, disturbed that a future Supreme Court justice would be so ignorant of a reality entangled in the body politic of this American social structure.

But the essence of black life does not influence how a white woman of Justice Barrett's status and stature should navigate the social terrain of the world, and no doubt, Justice Barrett, as a mother of two adopted black children, desires to remove social barriers for these black children by bringing them into a new world filled with elevated social opportunities and rights of excess and consumption. She perhaps believes her willingness to adopt and raise two black children indicates that she is invested in improving black life one child at a time. However, she may be committed to providing a better life for these children, a better life under the umbrella of her influence and protection. And so long as they keep the name Barrett and move and maneuver in ways their bequeathed privileges afford them advantages, which are tethered to a culturally protected name, they will be safe, secure, and prosperous.

One must ponder, however, what happens when the adopted children's black skin overshadows their white cultural affiliation by another white person who considers a black presumption of cultural standing to whiteness as an affront to their traditional heritage? Additionally, raising black children within a white social milieu, devoid of the proper balance and instruction of black culture and history, I surmise, creates black social cogs committed to keeping a certain elitism as devoted guardians of the status quo. In essence, such socially and culturally deprived individuals, rather than working to change the racial dysfunctions of society by way of agitation, become devoted to maintaining a system that assisted them to levels of social elevation.[4] Why, such individuals ask, tinker with something

---

4. As Peter Berger and Thomas Luckmann raise in the classic *The Social Construction of Reality*, all social constructions in the world derive from human notions and behavior. Humans, therefore, become definers, but what allows one to be a definer? All human beings could define reality, but realities are also defined within the confines of allotted personal and social spacing. In Cynthia D. Moe-Lobeda's *Resisting Structural Evil*, systemic injustice, to be remedied, must focus on probing for factors that cloak structural injustice "to the point of invisibility, the focus is not on the power dynamics that cause injustice, but more on the dynamics that cause us not to recognize it." Moe-Lobeda, *Resisting*, 87.

that works? Becoming devoted guardians of the status quo occurs by way of ignorance that one is being used as a pawn to limit blackness and elevate whiteness and by way of arrogance in believing that if one black has achieved greatness, despite the odds, every black has an equal opportunity to do the same.

III.

An excellent example in the arrogance category is seen in how former Kentucky Attorney General Daniel Cameron seems to look to elevate himself to a higher social status at the expense of telling the truth about the events surrounding the Breonna Taylor murder. Cameron reasons that being in a position of power, which he has due likely to white assistance and endorsement, could further his ambition by refusing to validate a criminal claim that would place undesired attention upon a particular political base, to which he owes his allegiance. After an unsuccessful gubernatorial run, Cameron became CEO of 1792 Exchange, where he vows to "continue meaningful work to put an end to the anti-America ESG agenda that threatens to take over our corporations and change the fabric of our country."[5] The fabric to which Cameron refers is seen in how intricately woven notions of anti-blackness are displayed in the tapestry of religion, education, and law (i.e., American society). The fabric to which he refers was also woven together to provide the covering of white legitimacy, and this fabric is undoubtedly well made; it holds its integrity without the probability of tearing or being ripped apart. This metaphorical garb has been used for centuries through generational inheritance. The only requirement to ensure its longevity is day-to-day maintenance, done with the utmost *Cameronian* pleasure.

An example of the ignorance (i.e., unknowing/negation) category is astrophysicist Neil deGrasse Tyson, a remarkably brilliant scholar and public intellectual who believes the modifier *black* is unnecessary when addressing his individualized talent and success, who once replied to a black man named Marc who wrote to him to learn the degree to which his experience as a black scientist showed strides of both tension and progression. After providing examples of his appointment to the 2001 White House commission to study the future of the US aerospace industry, Tyson attests critics merely associated his position as one of tokenism but argues that such a conclusion proved invalid as another black, a four-star air force

---

5. See Smith, "Outgoing Kentucky Attorney General," para. 4.

general, was also appointed on the twelve-member committee. Additionally, he recalls a time in 1996, a time that he also admits that he was not well known to the public, when his employer, the American Museum of Natural History, where he served as director of the Hayden Planetarium, held a gala in which a particular lady presumed he was in attendance in a community affairs capacity, a position Tyson identifies as a position reserved for "token Blacks." Tyson concludes by suggesting:

> Those kinds of encounters were common then, but simply do not occur anymore, except, possibly, among older people whose life experience was shaped in a Black & White America, rather than in simply, America. Various high-profile biographical mentions of me in recent years make no mention of my skin color. So, the trends don't support your contentions, or perhaps, it indicates that your experience does not represent prevailing trends and truths. Thank you for your supportive comments, and while the struggle continues, the times are indeed a-changin'.[6]

Unfortunately, the world in which Tyson ebbs and flows as an extraordinarily gifted man with black skin is a quasi-safe space. The lecture hall, fundraisers, privileged meetings, cocktail parties, and so on seem to be the extent to which he gauges levels of oppression for blackness. This is not to suggest that Tyson does not think about the various nuances of the struggle for black people in America or the world, for that matter. Instead, it is a suggestion that perhaps a certain level of individual accomplishment hinders, to a degree, the level of empathetic association with the lived experience of the average black within the context of knowing the depth and breadth of how the nature of intentional social barriers make it rather tricky for some blacks to have a glimmer of hope. It is indeed a fallacy to suggest that focus, grit, and discipline are all that one needs to be successful in the world—at least, I presume this to be the case for black people. I highly doubt that a racial epithet would be shouted at someone of Tyson's esteem in these culturally manicured spaces. Still, silence does not equate to unresponsiveness to an inherited cultural thought about the *other*. And even if he has achieved a certain level of acceptance within white space, there are unchartered dimensions that would reduce his achievements as a prolific scientist and intellectual to that of a social affront based merely on the color of his skin.

In *Woke Racism: How a New Religion Has Betrayed Black America*, John McWhorter, who somehow runs on a similar continuum as Tyson,

---

6. Tyson, *Letters*, 13–15.

takes issue with what he terms *Third Wave Antiracism*. Within this school of thought, there seems to be an aggressive and far-reaching condemnation of white people and their inherited possession of privilege, which exposes them to unwarranted notions of universal complicity in black oppression.[7] Much like McWhorter, I take issue with using the phrase *wokeness*, not its spirit of suggestion. My primary critique of its use is centered on my understanding and study of consciousness (i.e., awareness) as presented in religion, cosmology, spirituality, and neuroscience. However, I also understand that consciousness is both a subjective and objective experience regarding matters of racial analysis.

On a personal level, people who subscribe to the title of being *woke* tend to do so based on a particular moment of inflection in which one comes to terms with the reality of the given situation of universal oppression of blackness. For instance, a *woke* individual may devote time and energy to reading and studying the historical movement of black people and discover, at a fundamental level, that at every notable turn, black people are rebuffed and sequestered to limited social mobility. Thus, such individuals devote themselves to a sort of perennial awareness that manifests in the manner of dress, for instance, to display objectively that one is *aware* of cultural symbols of blacks such as African colors, garb, and vocabulary. Additionally, wearing the ancient Egyptian symbol *ANKH* is a beautiful illustration of this point because at the very core of these symbols lies a fundamental truth; that is, these African markers of meaning and significance are a reminder to the wearer and the observer that there is dignity and sophistication associated with black skin. This view counters the antithetical notion of Africans being devoid of dignity and sophistication before European engagement and influence.

In terms of wokeness, an inner awareness is to be manifested outwardly as a measure of denunciation of Western norms, and a direct appreciation for an African value and ethical system of existence. Being *woke*, or aware, is very much a central theme coursing throughout the black American experience. Even in writing *Woke Racism*, McWhorter is practicing *wokeness* to awaken in the individual, I presume both black and white, a sense of redirection and appreciation toward a more tenable solution to the race problem beyond merely alerting white people to their privilege. Moreover, McWhorter reasons that *wokeness* functions as a type of new religion. At the core of this belief system, salvation is obtainable when one (i.e., white

---

7. McWhorter, *Woke Racism*, 5.

people) accepts that the sins of their forebears somehow mysteriously become inserted into the everyday life world of white folk; thus, the need to repent and even perhaps practice penance by committing to providing financial assistance to antiracism programs, lowering social standards of acceptance, and feeling a sense of responsibly and complicity in furthering a racist social structure, implicitly and explicitly, become the measures by which one experiences the process of, dare I say, being born again.[8]

In the early twentieth century, however, Du Bois's uncanny ability to see how white people come to believe that racial supremacy is anchored in a particular yet uncritical belief and faith via modes of ethics and values, which are not subject to historical suspension, is undoubtedly worthy of illumination. Du Bois writes about a particular cultural/metaphoric religious adaptation that contradicts McWhorter's thesis of *wokeness* as a new religion. He describes the perennial quest for white dominance via the systematic control over education and every other part associated with social structuring as the *religion of whiteness*. Du Bois argues that whiteness, in and of itself, is a religiously devoted experience in which tenets of social mores and taboos are kept throughout society. Both *wokeness* and *whiteness* occupy the same theoretical terrain in describing the complicated and intricate nature of the human mind; therefore, behavior is somehow inextricably influenced by notions of historical memory regarding how people find meaning and come to exist in the social world. Considering the complicated social analysis associated with understanding how white people operate religiously regarding matters of cultural formations of identity, I must concur with Du Bois's position but also with the great Algerian psychiatrist and public intellectual Frantz Fanon, whose analytical work and summation of the problem of race and oppression in the world suggests that black people, by way of social conditioning, become utterly resentful toward white people, and on a deeper level, themselves.[9] Due to the extent of this resentment, miseducation, and the process of *othering*, it is essential to focus on fighting the disease of oppression rather than its symptoms to arrive at the *Thing* (i.e., the fundamental cause of the matter).

---

8. Spike Lee's *Do the Right Thing* and *School Daze* are both examples of a desire to awaken people to the reality of the abuse of marginalized black space, as well as the abuse of black people within the black sub-world who support Westernized practices of group formations and social respectability. In *School Daze*, for instance, the last line in the movie is repeated across the black social spectrum with an earnest plea: "Wake up."

9. Hayes, "Fanon."

One must consider history's guideposts when asking who we are and how we got here. Guideposts are those signs that tell us where we are, and they also tell us where we are going; strangely enough, they tell us where we have been. In one moment in time, we are connected at the intersection of all three experiences, which help shape and define who we are as human beings; yet, after following the progression of historical markers, which guides one to the reality of systemic oppression being the cause of black peoples' pain and suffering, one is left dumbfounded to learn that although an element of the *thing*, it is not the *Thing*. Racism is a significant guidepost, but it is not the *Thing*. In its contemporary use, racism is merely a symptom of a more sophisticated evil, and it is our ignorance and arrogance that prevent us from considering anything otherwise.

3

BETWEEN A ROCK AND A HARD PLACE
(The Origin of Black Compromise and Betrayal)

> Not only do white men but also colored men forget the facts of the Negro's double environment. The Negro American has for his environment not only the white surrounding world but also, and touching him usually much more nearly and compellingly, is the environment furnished by his own-colored group.[1]
>
> —W. E. B. Du Bois

WITHIN THE DEVELOPMENT OF the *New World* chattel slave system, the notion of freedom became a commonality within the hearts of Africans. Freedom within this context, however, is undoubtedly subjective in nature. For some enslaved Africans, freedom meant getting back to the essence of who they were as tribal and cultural beings. This desire required that they push back and reject the social label of being viewed solely as a commodity. To achieve this end, enslaved Africans often rebelled and killed their enslavers, and at times, they also killed compromising Africans who rejected the notion of rebellion. On the other hand, compromising Africans chose the freedom to engage in the *New World* economic system, which afforded a minuscule amount of black wealth to be obtained. Modern black society grapples with a similar social dynamic of power and the desire for control;

1. Du Bois, "Colored World," 681.

thus, some blacks, having the desire to carve more social and economic space in Western society, often become guilty of the very thing that they may claim white social structures have for centuries inflicted upon people that look like them.

This experience has a point-of-origin narrative that illuminates social characters that influence the generational transference of betrayal and compromised identity within a subsect of the black world; namely, such persons are identified as *watchdogs* (i.e., guardians, kidnappers, drivers, overseers, rowers, guilds, and domestics). Commencing in the 1400s, these compromising African peoples stand on the other side of blackness to carve more space for themselves within an emerging dominant white world while blocking spaces of advancement for other blacks who find themselves stuck between a rock, the white world domination system, and a hard place, a compromising black sub-world.

To be sure, Africans heavily influenced the initial development of *New World* chattel enslavement. Herman Bennett's *African Kings and Black Slaves* seriously cautions one not to be too presumptuous in notions regarding *absolute* European power and influence over Africans during this period.[2] The social unrest and instabilities of governments created space for African elites to rise to a newly elevated status of wealth, providing a broader context of power and control over the Upper Guinea Coast.[3] The African elite often determined the contractual agreement with European traders, including but not limited to the import of firearms to fuel the trade.[4] Eventually, West Coast African elites conspired with early traders to sell Africans for European goods. Trade became so advanced that forts and castles were initially constructed to defend against and protect European powers from one another. Still, at that exact moment, the slave trade began growing exponentially, and the forts, castles, and churches would eventually turn into slave dungeons.

Early European caravans did not make it to the forest hinterland without the guidance of many opportunistic Africans. No doubt, inroads were made without African guidance.[5] Still, I do not suspect the new endeavor of chattel enslavement would have been as long lasting or profitable without such guidance from opportunistic Africans. The earliest of this trend is

2. H. Bennett, *African Kings*, 6, 12.
3. H. Bennett, *African Kings*, 22.
4. H. Bennett, *African Kings*, 68.
5. See Park, *Travels into the Interior of Africa*.

with the Afro-Portuguese, the Tangomaos, who worked as intermediaries between European traders and Senegambian kingdoms.[6] The earliest *African Europeans*, forebears to African Americans, are developed in this same cultural expansion. Because of the well-oiled machine between merchants, raiders, and African royalty, whites were spared the trouble of hunting slaves in the bush. They only had to "sit and wait."[7]

As forts and castles were built along the West African coast, so were communities that resulted from the sexual exploits of this mixture of peoples. The presence of Europeans on the West Coast of Africa invariably created the probability of attraction between white European men and both willing and unwilling African women. African European families were formed because European men engaged in sexual intercourse with African women and eventually set up a community in which a mixed race of children and willing African women lived in relative peace as many Africans were shipped throughout the known *New World*. Homes crafted in the likeness of European architecture, such as São Jorge da Mina Castle communal space, supplied comfort to the mistress who gave birth to an African European male. These women were often safe from the luring hunger of enslavement. Thus, such privileged Africans were set aside as a new way of being both African and European in the *New World*.[8]

THE *NEW WORLD*, AFRICAN ELITE, AND COMPROMISING IDEALS

Between the middle 1400s and the mid to late 1800s, European slavers created a narrative of the new hybrid black as a subhuman specimen lacking wisdom, culture, knowledge, ingenuity, love, forbearance, proper religion and spirituality, values, and ethics within a context of a *New World* chattel system. This achievement was made possible through the willing cooperation of compromising hybrid blacks. However, some newly instituted uncompromising hybrid blacks held on to fragments of the tarnished tale of cosmic significance and passed this story, along with the developing

---

6. Barry, *Senegambia*, 41.
7. Barry, *Senegambia*, 63.
8. A church building named St. George was erected, and a chaplain was appointed to serve; eventually, as the European expansion increased off the West Coast of Africa, provisions were made to increase religious instruction from one chaplain to four. Sanneh, *West African Christianity*, 23.

updated version, down from one enslaved generation to the next. Within this newly constructed narrative, the compromising hybrid black is situated in a relational triangulation in which survival becomes highly complicated because of European traders' strong influence on the lived experience of the hybrid blacks, in general, within the sub-world.

As stated previously, slavery and the time shared between European men and vulnerable, and sometimes opportunistic, African women produced Atlantic Creoles. These European men discovered Africa's richness and began a trade system.[9] The trade was worth protecting, so Europeans strategically began setting up a focused watch and controlling this lucrative trading position. Forts and castles were security measures to maintain a position against other encroaching opportunistic Europeans. In the 1400s, children were born to European men and African women seeking a better life. The privileged children birthed into this new existence were educated in European ways; for instance, in 1722, the Danes[10] built a school for this new class of African Europeans at Christiansborg Castle, and a school was also constructed at Pokeso.[11] By the 1740s, an African slave, Johannes Eliza Capitein, was educated at the University of Leyden and would go on to speak before audiences regarding the matter of theological proof for the advocacy and divine approval of African enslavement.[12]

The children of this early new class proved beneficial as they created another layer that substantiated European normalcy reflected upon the world—an abuse of power and privilege. The transition from the commodities of African goods to the commodity of African bodies transformed forts and castles into dungeons. As areas grew, for instance, "in 1555 Cape Coast counted only twenty houses; by 1680 it had 500 or more,"[13] so did the sexual urges of the European man, and relationships turned into communities where the descendants of these unions also became resources for slavers to use to further supplant a stronghold on the trade of Africans.

The new elite of African Europeans also took part in factory life on the Guinea Coast. They worked as gangs. For instance, "there was a gang man

---

9. "Factories or *feitorias* that European expansionists established along the coast of Africa in the fifteenth century." Berlin, *Many Thousands Gone*, 18.

10. The Danes built the last of the Gold Coast forts in 1787 at Fort Aygustaborg at Teshi. See Van Dantzig, *Forts and Castles*, 58.

11. Abuka, *House of Slaves*, 12–19.

12. Van Dantzig, *Forts and Castles*, 66.

13. Van Dantzig, *Forts and Castles*, 66.

to every twenty enslaved people, and they took turns through the night standing guard, with whips, to keep order."[14] Duties also included head shaving, washing, and branding, and seeing to it that the blacks were duly secured every night to posts driven in the ground. Slave ship captains also hired Gold Coast Africans to train newly enslaved Africans to be guardians and overseers. The guardians would sleep among the enslaved people and proudly use violence to restore order. They were to settle quarrels, organize eating groups, supervise work parties, and detect rebellion plots. In 1808, aboard the *Coralline*, African overseer Shakoe, as it happens, was accustomed to taking his frustrations out on the enslaved. One day, the enslaved people attacked without much notice and beat his brains out.[15] Violent occasions such as the Shakoe incident would become ordinary engagement opportunities for compromising Africans and enslaved, uncompromising Africans for many years to come.

The *Watchdogs*, as they were called, were given a better life as compromising enslaved people rather than protesting enslaved people. The compromising slave's job was to keep and secure the newly enslaved African way of being. The enslaved had to fight European dominance while also grappling with what would become an equally daunting black betrayal. Betrayal was undoubtedly experienced in the differentiated world of African society and politics, so the notion of unified slave consciousness may present as problematic for some. Nevertheless, such a phenomenon does exist. One can see, for instance, this dialectical dance with the Coromantee Africans from the Gold Coast.

The Coromantee spawned from the Akan peoples (i.e., Asante, Ga, Fanti, Akwama, and Denkyira). Europeans knew the history of the Coromantee as being that of intense and determined warriors. Because of their physical prowess and military soundness, it is no wonder that early Europeans seized on an opportunity to reduce the probability of rebellions by selecting the strongest, the Coromantee, as managers of oppression, as it were. European slavers left nothing to chance; they provided the strategically selected managers and awarded them more food, clothing, possessions, and suitable living quarters.

Indeed, some Coromantees decided to use their gifts of combat training to enhance the power and authority of Europeans over their own Coromantee brothers and sisters. Still, there are occasions where one views just

14. Dow, *Slave Ships and Slaving*, 212.
15. E. Taylor, *If We Must Die*, 78, 105.

the opposite. Their long history of fighting against Europeans also provides evidence of this fact. For instance, two hundred Coromantee enslaved persons, in 1673, rebelled against Lobby's plantation in St. Ann's Parish and killed whites, took up arms, and fled to the mountains.[16] The Coromantee also led rebellions in Barbados in 1675, the Danish island of St. John in 1733, Antigua in 1736, Jamaica in 1760, Berbice in 1763, and Guyana in 1823.[17]

MOMENTS OF BETRAYAL

While military aggression continued to supply an assortment of Africa's most well-developed bodies, merchants, in cahoots with kidnappers and raiders, pushed from the other end.[18] Between 1757 and 1806, 64,828 guns were imported from Europe.[19] With the aid of so-called *Watchdogs*, this use of advanced arms made slave-raiding even more profitable. The movement of *black commodities* along the treacherous march to the coast included guilds and African European traders, such as the notorious Jan Niezer.[20]

Betrayal simply translated into economic gain.[21] Betrayal also had its obvious advantage, freedom. In 1704, aboard the *Eagle*, during a revolt, slaves nearly tossed the captain and crew overboard. Rebels hit the captain with a piece of wood and were going to hit him again but were hindered when a fellow slave intervened and blocked the blow with his arm, breaking it. The ship's doctor treated the slave, who was granted freedom upon his arrival in Virginia.[22] In 1767, aboard the Danish slave ship *Fredensborg*, Akwambo slaves were betrayed by an African woman. I presume this betrayal was motivated by the African woman developing a sense of loyalty to her enslavers.

Additionally, Ewes on the coast were not averse to selling Ewes from the interior. Notions of community often did not extend beyond a group of villages or towns in a particular area. A "free negro," Captain Peter Tongerloe, had a small plantation with nine slaves overlooking Christiansted. A

16. Craton, *Testing the Chains*, 76.
17. Craton, *Testing the Chains*, 61.
18. Berlin, *Many Thousands Gone*, 100–101.
19. Inikori, "Import," 142–43.
20. Van Dantzig, *Forts and Castles*, 69.
21. Aptheker, *American Negro*, 59.
22. E. Taylor, *If We Must Die*, 107.

female slave was captured by blacks, sold to a black man on St. Croix, and finally bought by the free black Tongerloe.[23] To address the issue of betrayal, during the Muslim rebellion in Bahia, "Word on the exact date only reached the rank and file a few days beforehand. This security measure was employed to reduce any likelihood of betrayal as much as possible."[24] And compromising blacks on occasion met a brutal end as a result of betrayal. In 1748, enslaved Africans in South Carolina conspired to kill all the whites within the vicinity, set the town ablaze, and killed all blacks who refused to join the rebellion.[25]

IT (*BE*) YOUR OWN PEOPLE

From beginning to end, the practice of Africans kidnapping Africans was a significant element in how Europeans went about acquiring black bodies. Europeans referred to slave catchers, or kidnappers, as *Siccadingers,* black gold. With wealth, African kidnappers, for instance, Kpego, Babatu, and Samori, were able to establish standing armies as a means of raiding and causing actions of war, which were all used to acquire more slaves to sell.[26] A famous kidnapper, Ben Johnson, was very powerful and wielded much influence over the region, which was off *Piccaninni Sestus* on the Windward Coast.[27] The Fon and Asante were especially active participants in the abduction, trading, buying, selling, and shipping of Africans.[28] Moreover, Foulahs in the Town of Bondou aided the enslavement of Africans by supplying provisions for coffles,[29] and in the later eighteenth century, Mandinga chiefs developed slave towns. Indeed, Mandingos, Susus, and Fulas controlled the upper Guinea trade and provided space in which Europeans would benefit from African-on-African *New World* slaving practices.[30]

The Mandinka *Slatees* were elite African merchants who ventured deep into the interior to buy prisoners and sell goods obtained from

---

23. E. Taylor, *If We Must Die*, 193.
24. Reis, *Slave Rebellion in Brazil*, 116.
25. Horne, *Counter-Revolution*, 157.
26. A. Bailey, *African Voices*, 61, 80–81, 86.
27. Mannix and Cowley, *Black Cargoes*, 92.
28. Hurston, *Barracoon*, xvi; Rediker, *Slaveship*, 98.
29. Rediker, *Slaveship*, 46.
30. Rodney, "African Slavery."

Europeans on the coast.[31] In West Central Africa, the *Bobangi* fishermen were known for their attachment to and profit from the trade.[32] The coastal tribes had *Krumen*, expert fishermen boat navigators with superb physical physiques and dark black skin.[33] The process of African enslavement became so unpredictable that even the so-called elite, if not ever vigilant, found themselves, the co-constructers of the system, also caught up in the fray. For instance, the *remidors* were African rowers,[34] and an African seaman, Amissa, while rowing slaves ashore in Jamaica, soon discovered that he had also been sold.[35]

As the European slavers called them, drivers were used to socializing the remaining slaves to the new rank and file in the *New World*. This early differentiation of the enslaved Africans was ingenious. The slaves hated the African drivers to such a degree that on some occasions, when most of the slaves rebelled, the African driver, rather than fighting with Africans, chose to remain loyal to the financier. However, there are instances in which a driver would put down the whip and join his fellow captured Africans. In 1823, driver Telemachus understood the error of his ways and refused to inflict further harm on the enslaved. He was demoted as a result and whipped severely. His rise as a rebel leader was likely due to empathy toward people who looked like him.[36]

In the British West Indies, slaves working as domestics became the first black scholars within the slave community. It is likely such individuals received their sense of worth from the teachings of the *Slave Bible,* a source that researcher Joseph Lumpkin refers to as the world's most outstanding example of a social manipulation tool.[37] Nevertheless, they were the closest to the subject, the white world. They were the first to learn the language and the first black ethnography experts; for all intents and purposes, they became immersed in European ways of thinking and doing. Because whites considered slaves unimpressive intellectually, they spoke rather openly in the presence of these domestics, some of whom would suppress feelings

---

31. Alford, *Prince*, 23.
32. Rediker, *Slaveship*, 94–97.
33. Mannix and Cowley, *Black Cargoes*, 16.
34. Mannix and Cowley, *Black Cargoes*, 16.
35. Christopher, *Slave Ship Sailors*, 61.
36. E. Taylor, *If We Must Die*, 54–55.
37. Lumpkin, "Introduction," xxiv.

and would use their position of privilege, at times, to collect information and pass it along to the field hands.[38]

Domestics, males and females, were afforded the most prestigious position a slave could obtain within the structural confines of chattel enslavement. Particular slaves were chosen to function as servants of the house, a position allotting them to serve a family member for their life. This was an honor for many slaves and a dishonor for many others. The Newton Plantation in Barbados was a place where the name Old Doll carried much influence and power; despite being a domestic slave, Old Doll was considered the crème de la crème of the slave community. Her half-sister, Mary Ann, had a standing sexual relationship with a white man who extended his privilege and willed Mary Ann a slave named Esther.[39] Out of this social arrangement, the ruling class obtained loyalists who would function as spies and alert whites to any nefarious ramblings amidst the black community.[40] As a result of this abuse of black power and privilege, Henry Bibb reasoned, "This is one of the principal causes of the slaves being divided among themselves, and without which they could not be held in bondage one year, and perhaps not half that time."[41]

FRAGMENTED BLACK SOCIETY
(*Black Skin Abhors Black Skin*)

By 1790, South Carolina had set up an elite class of free blacks, which, much like their Atlantic Creole cousins, desired to work within the social structure of a slave system and profit rather than fight against it and lose everything. They referred to themselves as the Brown Fellowship Society. Whether enslaved or free, dark-skinned people were prohibited. This is one of the earliest organized measures on North American soil related to the quest for black social mobility within a racially unjust society.

> The Brown Fellowship Society fragmented black society by excluding slaves and dark-skinned free people.[42] Before long, dark-

---

38. Craton, *Testing the Chains*, 44.
39. Beckles, *Natural Rebels*, 67.
40. Beckles, *Natural Rebels*, 67.
41. Beckles, *Natural Rebels*, 62. David Walker, that fierce rebel against enslavement of blacks, also concluded that major deterrents to black liberation were black traitors and spies. See Walker, *David Walker's Appeal*, 46.
42. The Brown Fellowship Society in South Carolina also aided some slaves to buy

skinned people established a similar association, the Humane Brotherhood. Thus did the color divisions that supported slavery became suffused throughout the black community: what whites did to browns, browns did to blacks.[43]

A slave known as Antonio, a Negro, was sold to the Bennett family. It is unclear as to what prompted Antonio, a Negro, to garner the type of favor he received from whites. He may have fought and survived an Indian raid that killed many just a year later. He was allowed to marry and farm his food while still a slave; eventually, favor extended to Antonio, a Negro, and his family was given their freedom. Antonio, a Negro, became Anthony Johnson. He also became a wealthy man through his connection to bringing servants and future slaves into North America. His sons would carry on the generational practice of holding slaves as a means of securing financial wealth.[44]

By the 1840s, William Alexander Leidesdorff, a free man, hid the fact his father was white and that his mother was from the Virgin Islands. He navigated white space as a white man because his complexion, although ancestrally black, allowed him to do so. He could also learn, apply, and adapt to white cultural norms. When Mexico declared war on the United States, although he lived in Mexican territory then, he became a compromising American diplomat.[45]

After four centuries of producing a hybrid class of blacks and seducing compromising Africans, Europeans, then American whites, could rest well in knowing the results of such an agenda to create a hybrid black with a morbid sense of personality.[46] While early enslaved blacks attempted to rectify their social situations with rebellion, such attempts were often thwarted not by white slavers alone but by blacks to whom they were chained and by blacks who watched over them to ensure they stayed situated in their state of oppression. One would have to deduce that compromising slaves observed an opportunity to elevate themselves above their problem of having black skin by aligning with the social movement of the *New World*. The

---

freedom. See R. Bailey, *Neither Carpetbaggers nor Scalawags*, 55.

43. R. Bailey, *Neither Carpetbaggers nor Scalawags*, 342.
44. R. Bailey, *Neither Carpetbaggers nor Scalawags*, 29–30.
45. Wills, *Black Fortunes*, 4.
46. Du Bois published "The Religion of the American Negro" (1900). This essay would be edited and republished in *The Souls of Black Folk* (1903). See Du Bois, *On Sociology*, 222.

objective was clear whether guardian, driver, fisherman, kidnapper, overseer, merchant, or domestic. One survives blackness by sacrificing others with black skin in hopes that the constant feeding machine of *New World* chattel slavery would consider such a gesture as an act of acquiescence; ultimately, the uncompromising people with black skin stuck in the middle of this social circumstance would become the sacrificial lambs.

4

TOWARD A *NEW WORLD*
(*Pawns of Commerce and the New Enterprise of Chattel Slavery*)

THE *NEW WORLD*, OR birth and wealth building of European civilization, began in the fifteenth century. Before this infamous moment, the Moors (i.e., North African Muslims) ruled parts of Spain for eight hundred years, commencing in 711, and contributed significantly to the cultural and technological advancement of the region. African empires such as Songhay also had world-renowned intellectual spaces at the University of Sankore. Additionally, Africans traded and engaged in commerce with Spain, Italy, and the Eastern Roman Empire.[1] However, during the Middle Ages, direct contact between West Africa and Europe was limited, and European avarice and African vulnerability at some juncture further severed this once mutually beneficial relationship.[2] The initial European pursuit and confiscation of lands to the East was not for harvesting precious metals or capturing black bodies. It was the trade in spices, silks, colorful clothing, tea, coffee, and alcohol that motivated the European movement.

While making such a movement, however, Spain and Portugal became aware of the potential economic opportunities of inordinate wealth if they commandeered vast amounts of silver and gold, respectively, in Africa.[3]

---

1. Du Bois, *World and Africa*, 44.
2. Du Bois, *World and Africa*, 46.
3. Du Bois, *World and Africa*, 46.

While traversing the valleys of the Ankobra and Volta Rivers, for instance, Martin Fernandes and Alvaro Esteves became enthused when they discovered gold in those lands in 1471.[4] Columbus was undoubtedly elated to have received news of the land southwest of Cape Verde Islands, and blacks traded with an "African alloy of gold called guanin."[5] Africa's significant quantity of gold attracted Mediterranean areas since the Byzantine era,[6] and, as Toby Green makes clear in *A Fistful of Shells*, on the Gold Coast in particular, for nearly two centuries, there was no established export slave trade between these Portuguese Europeans and Africans. It was African traders such as the *dyula* who typically bought enslaved Africans outside of the Gold Coast region. And it is these Africans from the Kingdom of Benin that the *dyula* used to carry European goods north and carry mined gold to the coast. Green also notes that Africans were used as beasts of the field because they were the best option to combat the tsetse fly, an insect that killed most *beasts of burden* in the dense African forest.[7]

The high and profitable consumption of these commodities, especially gold, and a quest to do away with an untenable labor force place Africa in peril, as it had been selected as the most practical target due to the other option, people in the Americas, being poorly suited to take on such a demanding task of forced manufacturing labor. It is safe to suggest those privileged individuals wearing the clothes, drinking tea, coffee, and alcohol, and smoking tobacco were doing so at the expense of human beings torn from their families, physically abused, and, on many accounts, worked to literal death, for the sole purpose of creating European wealth. And Europeans fought among themselves to claim the fame of global dominance.

I.

The African and European relationship was not strained from the outset; however, Europeans and Africans first had a long trade and commerce history.[8] In fact, Africans and mulattoes went with European explorers to the

---

4. Anquandah, *Castles and Forts*, 14.
5. Du Bois, *Gift of Black Folk*, 5–9.
6. Thornton, *Africa and Africans*, 26.
7. Green, *Fistful of Shells*, 118.
8. There are several avenues to take about the analysis of how the African slave trade began or originated; one avenue I advocate investigating as a point of departure is the black plague of Europe between 1347 and 1350, also known as the Black Death. The

Americas as early as the 1490s, and in 1537, Cortes took three hundred blacks with him when he claimed the land known as California. The Canary Islands, as a point of departure for both African and European exploratory factions, commenced in the early 1300s and provided an excellent scope of potentiality for future profits. Furthermore, although it has been suggested that African slavery is equally responsible for the external Atlantic slave trade, one must note that African notions of slavery were vastly different from the new form of human bondage that was experienced by Africans in *New World* chattel enslavement.

The objective in fifteenth-century Europe was to increase the demand and profitability of manufacturing goods. The high demand for sugar, for instance, transitioned causal kidnapping cases from Africans and the acquisition of African war captives to an all-out assault of any African within reach of Europeans. Foreign relations between Africa and European nations took a tremendous shift when European powers realized the margins of profitability in scaling the business of manufacturing goods by placing substantial attention on producing free labor, the building and supplying a crew of a slave ship, for instance, was a business expense associated with such a production. A new business model was developed, and more liquidity was directed toward increasing free labor due to the high demand for goods. Thus, people with black skin become the conduit through which Europe elevates itself from the catastrophic experience of the black plague during the middle 1300s, the Hundred Years' War, and famine.[9]

II.

Although the plantation system emerged as a means of economic exploitation that began in the 1300s along the Atlantic islands (i.e., Azores, Madeiras, Canaries, and Cape Verde), the addition of owning, selling, physically branding, rape, and sometimes murder, created an adapted way of slaving within the confines of the structure of the *New World*. From 1340 to 1470,

---

European population was depleted, and resources were needed to improve their social plight. Another point to consider is the pilgrimage of Mansa Musa of Mali, who traveled to Mecca in 1324–25 and displayed possessing copious amounts of gold. He gave so much away along his journey that economic systems would collapse. The desperation for wealth, the need for resources, and calculated opportunity would eventually entice some Africans to join forces with European powers.

9. See L. Bennett, *Before the Mayflower*, 32–33.

European expansion along the coast of Africa was slow but steady,[10] and then the Treaty of Tordesillas divided the *New World* between Spain and Portugal in 1494.[11] As it happened, one European superpower said to the other, *you go that way, and we will go this way*. As time passed and European powers fought for economic global control, notions of religion and wealth-building consumed the lands of millions of people, with the continent of Africa being its primary target in the *New World*.

The *New World*, as seen in the minds of early ambitious Europeans, translated into exploits of exploration that focused on the potential wealth found in lands beyond their locales. "The Portuguese, under Bartholomew Diaz, rounded the Cape of Good Hope in February 1448 and anchored in Mossel Bay."[12] The *New World*, especially as seen in the movement of early explorers and religious leaders such as Columbus, Cortes, Bernardino de Sahagún, and Las Casas, developed and expanded to accommodate the desire for human wealth and the consumption of goods via modes of religion and law;[13] and as this desire increased across Europe and the expanding world, African kingdoms were manipulated to go to war with other African kingdoms to justify the taking of war prisoners and selling them as slaves to opportunistic Europeans.

Backed by authentic religious decree, the *New World* chattel enslavement was directed toward the African slave trade, which sees its horrendous influence upon the lives of the enslaved Africans in Brazil, the Caribbean, and, to a lesser degree, North America, during the seventeenth century, which would be exacerbated due to demand for more sugar during the 1650s. Religion no doubt substantiated and blessed the voyages that would improve their social circumstances by providing, in the words of an early Spanish conquistador, Bernal Díaz del Castillo, an opportunity to "serve God and the king and also to get rich."[14] The papal bull *Romanus Pontifex*, sealed in 1455, provided the legal sanction from the church for Portugal, a

---

10. L. Bennett, *Before the Mayflower*, 32.

11. It is believed that the first white man to reach Benin was a Portuguese, Ruy de Sequeira, in 1472. Between 1441 and 1444, two hundred enslaved Africans were sent to Portugal. As a result of Prince Henry's explorations, by 1474 an estimated eight hundred slaves served as domestic servants every year.

12. Morris, *Washing of the Spears*, 18.

13. See Todorov, *Conquest of America*; Long, *Significations*, 110.

14. Palmer, *Slaves of the White God*, 65.

Christian church with significant African influence, to enslave all desired African peoples south of Cape Bojador.[15]

Three additional pivotal religious/legal points should be noted when considering significant measures used to anchor blacks in this new enterprise of chattel enslavement.

First, by reversing the old method of conferring the legal status of the father to the child, *Partus Sequitur Ventrem* ensured that the mother was to be considered the funnel by which a black person was socially constructed as a slave.[16] Second, traveling with a Moroccan expedition seeking to subdue Songhay to spread the Muslim faith tradition further into Africa's interior, in 1614 Aḥmad Bābā, an Islamic scholar from Timbuktu who lived from 1556 to 1627, wrote the seminal text on the matter of slavery, the *Mi raj al-Su'ud ila Nayl Hukm majlub al-Sud*.[17] In this text, translated as *The Ladder of Ascent Towards Grasping the Law Concerning Transported Blacks*, he condemned the enslavement of Muslims likely because of his own experience. Still, he insisted that if enslaved in unbelief, enslavement is duly justified.[18] Such a religious/political movement and propaganda no doubt influenced African enslavement on a much larger scale.[19] Third, and most significant, the monopoly system of the *New World*.

III.

The Spanish crown introduced the asiento (monopoly system) for extracting and importing slaves into the *New World*.[20] The Spanish/Portuguese were not alone. The Dutch, French, British, Prussians, Danes, and Swedes would eventually all become actively engaged in the African slave trade through negotiation between themselves, violence, and capitulation to European top dominance (i.e., asiento). As movement in the *New World*

15. H. Bennett, *African Kings*, 83. See Oden, *How Africa Shaped the Christian Mind*.
16. Darity and Mullen, *From Here to Equality*, 70–73.
17. Darity and Mullen, *From Here to Equality*, 31.
18. Lovejoy, "Context of Enslavement."
19. Many blacks in colonies from 1619 to the 1660s were contract servants. In Virginia by 1670, the House of Burgesses decided that servants who were not Christians were to become slaves for life. A practice known as pawnship was a choice for several affluent Africans as security for debts. Often, children fulfilled this role. Legally, a pawn could not be sold or traded. They were an investment. See Lovejoy, *Transformations in Slavery*, 13.
20. Palmer, *Slaves of the White God*, 9.

increased, it is argued that the Bantu destroyed the peace of the African empires. After this, the Mohammedans looked to take advantage of the chaos by raiding lands and taking Africans for harems and soldiers of their armies. European slavers advanced the agenda of exploitation by cunningly instigating war as a means of securing more slave labor for their expanding colonies.[21] Africans in the Kongo, for instance, were using Portuguese soldiers in 1514.[22]

Like the empire of Rome, African nations collapsed because of internal and external conflict.[23] Daniel Richter notes that the English aristocracy was descendants of tyrannical *strong men* who terrorized the region since the decline and fall of the Roman Empire and Charlemagne's fall. These men became powerful because they could afford private armies in exchange for protection.[24] The loss of imperial control by the defeated Romans left many people vulnerable to more forceful and powerful elements of human society, and they found themselves under the woeful band of slavery. Anglo Saxons from Germany and Holland forcefully raided England and eventually took possession of the land.[25]

The notion of slavery, or human bondage,[26] was a Roman ideal that was transmitted into a new cultural landscape in England. Chattel slavery was, however, a different social experience in a *New World* context. In sum, as noted by scholars, European slavery was a business with a particular way of existing.[27] Eventually, the English would undertake to secure the trade in 1562 through the activities of Sir John Hawkins. The European colonies

21. Woodson, *Negro in Our History*, 16.

22. Woodson, *Negro in Our History*, 41.

23. The northern coastline of Africa has been in contact with Europeans across the Mediterranean dating back to Greco-Roman times. There have been connections between Africans and Europeans for some established time prior to what we know to be the 1619 experience. See Abuka, *House of Slaves*, 79. And, according to Ivan van Sertima, there was an encounter between the Portuguese (i.e., Cadamosto's expedition) and Africans who greeted them with bows, although not initially, on the Gambia River in 1455. This is the first documented European description of African riverboats prior to Columbus's voyages. See Van Sertima, *They Came Before Columbus*, 52–54.

24. Richter, *Before the Revolution*, 42.

25. Inikori, "Slavery in Africa," 42.

26. Richter, *Before the Revolution*, 73. The words *slave* in English, *esclavo* in Spanish, and *esclave* in French all derive from the same root as *slav*, referring to the Eastern European peoples who were most commonly bought and sold in the late medieval period.

27. Barry, *Senegambia*, 48. Dutch West India Company (1625), French West India (1664), and Royal African Company (1672).

of North America would also make a drastic shift in the tradition of chattel enslavement beginning in the 1690s.

To make this new economic enterprise of chattel slavery as seamless as possible, castles and forts were built on African soil as initial modes of European protection from other encroaching European powers and trading purposes and, making inroads with the local African elites and traders in efforts to occupy African soil from the shoreline into the unforgiving hinterland forests. With guns and religion, Europeans placed a stamp of blessing on their *New World* endeavors by asserting notions of manifest destiny as legally permissible.

IV.

With brute intentionality and European aggression, the taking of *New World* lands was quite a methodical process.[28] The African slave trade was focused on Angola, and down a short 250-mile coastline, Europeans occupied space on black soil. As a move of strategic positioning, over several centuries of the Atlantic slave trade, Europeans built forts, castles, and dungeons to protect themselves and their investments in a new economy. The Portuguese carved space for themselves on the Gold Coast, and a fort was built with the blessing of God.[29] Elmina, named *the mine* by King Alphonso V, was built on the Gold Coast in 1482.[30] Eventually, thirty-three forts aligned with five major slave routes, Kumasi being the central point of departure from which many enslaved Africans were forced to march down to slave forts, were constructed.

The building of forts along the West African coast shows that European explorers and nations saw value in what the land could offer regarding resources. Empty land is profitable to the degree that one can build and occupy space, but the resources create wealth in occupied spaces. Forts and castles were not initially built to house slaves in these occupied lands.[31]

---

28. "Feudal dreams drove the string of conquests that followed as conquistadors poured out of their Hispaniola in 1501, Puerto Rico in 1508, Jamaica in 1509, and Cuba in 1511, and, on the mainland, the territories of the Aztecs in 1521, the Incas in 1536, and Chile in 1541." Richter, *Before the Revolution*, 50.

29. Abuka, *House of Slaves*, 78–79.

30. Anquandah, *Castles and Forts*, 14.

31. Edmund Abuka contends that upon reflection of the Middle Passage as a dynamic, transformative experience, one should be inclined to consider the fort, castle, and dungeon as critical factors in the transformation of the African human into a commodified

Instead, these European-constructed spaces were designed for rest, trade, and protection from other European trading factories in the late fifteenth and early sixteenth centuries.[32] These commerce spaces also stored goods for sale and held African goods purchased on the Gold Coast. In exchange for slaves, Europeans used items such as cowries, colorful cloth, firearms, iron, beads, and toys. Before the exportation of black bodies, Africans used West African commodities such as wax, hides, wood, gum, pepper, ivory, and gold for commercial exchange.[33]

Between 1505 and 1510, the Spanish colonies saw a transition to one sole commodity for the trade, and that was the African, rather than the people from the Iberian kingdoms; by 1510, King Ferdinand authorized the shipping of 250 Africans to Hispaniola, thus initiating the battle between European powers for wealth and the resource that would ensure this end (i.e., control of the African slave trade).[34] Moreover, the enslavement of Central Africans by the Portuguese increased after 1575 when Paulo Dias de Novias arrived in Angola.[35] African bodies were filtered through Luanda, Benguela, and Cabinda in West Central Africa. In the Bight of Benin, Quidah was the dreaded destination, and in the Bight of Biafra, Bonny also became known as a notorious slave port.[36] Quidah, however, was the central hub for the slave trade and selling, especially from the 1670s through the 1860s.[37] In 1509, the Spanish imported African slaves to Jamaica.[38]

The expansion of wealth also prompted an African response, in which some opportunistic Africans became investors in a newly crafted

---

piece of flesh. He, along with other scholars, for instance, Kwesi J. Anquandah, argues that the fort, castle, and dungeon "were slave ships at permanent sea." Forts also had a well-organized system of communal responsibility. Everyone working in specific areas, from the director general to the council, chief merchant, bookkeeper, works superintendent, chaplain, physician, schoolteacher, nurses, cooks, tailors, masons, carpenters, and garrison members, every duty contributed to the goal of supporting a place and space of business. See Abuka, *House of Slaves*, 40; Anquandah, *Castles and Forts*, 14.

32. By the seventeenth century, the first slave trading corporations were the Dutch West India Company (1621) and Royal African Company-English (1672). See Woodson, *Negro in Our History*, 21.

33. Abuka, *House of Slaves*, 4–18.

34. Restall, "Black Conquistadors."

35. Thornton, "Central Africa," 89.

36. Lovejoy, *Transformations in Slavery*, 129.

37. "In 1720s, Whydah became Dahomey's major port of trade." Anquandah, *Castles and Forts*, 104. See also Law, "William's Fort."

38. Craton, *Testing the Chains*, 67.

dog-eat-dog world. Accomplished to a degree with the aid of both armed and unarmed black conquistadors,[39] social freedom and the ability to thrive in a *New World* society are what inspired enslaved black conquistadors to join the European slave trade. Most of the black conquistadors were indeed born in Africa. They did not reach the Americas as a contingent of a European military force until spending time in Spain, Portugal, or one of the Caribbean colonies, after completing a tenure of faithful and devoted service to helping Europeans kill, pillage, and plunder native territories. However, some were not officially freed from bondage but nevertheless saw an improvement in their social lives.[40] However, the economic structure of chattel slavery would prove to be much more lucrative for white investment parties.

By the 1800s, Thomas Piketty argues, "slave holders in the New World controlled more wealth than the landlords of old Europe. Their farmland was not worth much, but since they had the bright idea of owning not just the land but also the labor force needed to work that land, their total capital was even greater."[41] Interestingly enough, based on Judah P. Benjamin's speech to the US Senate in 1860, *New World* slavery was valued at $4 billion; by 2019, it was calculated to be worth $42.2 trillion.[42] It can be argued that although some slave owners in this initial period worked alongside slaves in the field, the social power was imbalanced as the owners were free to maneuver in a way that created the best opportunity for their lives. The enslaved were hindered from developing and taking part in opportunities that afforded a better life for themselves. The owner was not working to ease the burden of the enslaved. Instead, the owner worked to help speed up the production process for commodities to sell or use to promote generational wealth. Additionally, white slave owners, African merchants, and government officials, especially those of royal lineage, such as kings, queens, and princes, took part in the internal and external trade of African

---

39. Woodson, *Negro in Our History*, 19–20.

40. Juan Garrido was given freedom, opportunity to gainful employment, and physical space in Mexico City. Sebastian Toral was given freedom and was exempt from paying tribute. Although Pedro Fulupo fought with the aspiration of a quid pro quo, it is unknown as to whether he ever received some form of recompense. Juan Bardales was given freedom with a pension totaling fifty pesos. And Juan Valiente was treated as if he was free. He would also gain status as a captain, and was granted an estate and an encomienda. See Woodson, *Negro in Our History*, 19–20.

41. Piketty, *Capital*, 199.

42. Darity and Mullen, *From Here to Equality*, 261.

bodies. Like other African exports used by merchants and government officials, the slave market was seen to be a substantial financial means to an end, and typically, underprivileged Africans would become the pawns of commerce and exchange in the *New World*.[43]

---

43. Lovejoy, *Transformations in Slavery*, 107.

5

THE SLAVE SHIP EXPERIENCE
(*A Beautiful Struggle*)

BLACKNESS, AS A CULTURAL phenomenon, was birthed at the precise moment newly enslaved Africans were shackled together in the belly of the slave ship, and the process of enslavement captured a dynamic new meaning. Thus, it is essential to reflect upon such a monumental event. Some captured Africans chose to fight for liberation in the barracoons, as well as during the dreadful trek known as the *death march*.[1] The slave ship experience, however, is of most import as it reveals a magnified psychological disruption within the black lived experience. This thought does not suggest that initial captivity for the Africans was a harmless experience; instead, I situate the slave ship experience at the center because this space of oppression was, for many, a time in which psychological wherewithal collapsed.

---

1. I consider the canoe experience a vital element in analyzing the slave ship experience. The canoes were small introductions to the experience that would eventually become the end destination, the slave ship. Two captured Africans would be situated on the floor of the canoe with arms tied behind their backs, and the rebellious ones would also have their knees constrained. The slavers learned early in the African slave trade to remove the captured Africans from the land expeditiously to decrease the volume and probability of protest and rebellion. Once shackled together, enslaved Africans could no longer concern themselves with past animosities about tribal conflict; instead, the here-and-now moment demanded that they survive, and the probability of survival grew exponentially under the auspices of the newly bonded slave community. These communal slaves shared a common religious heritage of suffering.

THE SLAVE SHIP EXPERIENCE

Death became the most expedient way in which to reconnect to the African cosmos and end the misery of their captivity. Interestingly enough, suicide was a means to restore one to the former state of blissful existence. The slaves who, however, survived the two-to-three-month voyage across the Atlantic did so by forming a bond with other enslaved Africans; thus, a once culturally differentiated group of oppressed peoples became *black* people. By the thirteenth century, as Joseph Holloway notes, Europeans were referring to all peoples from the African continent as African; that is, the unified oneness of black skin.[2]

The Portuguese designed the first African slave ship in the late 1400s. It was a full-rigged, round ship, three-masted craft with cannon-carrying capability for protection, communication, and intimidation. The more advanced form of protecting the investment of slave bodies was to communicate intimidation once away from the shore, so some officials would feed sharks along their paths to deflect attempts of Africans jumping overboard—the African will, nevertheless, would test the stretch of such intimidation by jumping into the shark-infested waters.[3] The early slave ship[4] en route to Mexico between 1570 and 1650 was relatively small, designed to carry 120 and 200 slaves, but that capacity was often superseded to accommodate 400 or 500 slaves.[5] To add insult to injury, these unholy vessels were named to convey divine right and ordination. *The Gift of God*, *Jesus*, and *Justice* are the most symbolically appalling examples.[6]

Words and phrases such as *horrible, sadistic,* and *unfathomable suffering* are ways of capturing the inarticulable experience that enslaved Africans endured within the belly of that horrid wooden abyss referred to as the slave ship. Every possible aid and spiritual channel was evoked in this place with yells, moans, screams, and depressive silence.[7] African life

---

2. See Holloway, *Africanisms*, xix.

3. Rediker, *Slaveship*, 39–42.

4. The typical slave ship had a captain, a first mate, a doctor, a carpenter, a boatswain, a gunner (or armorer), often a cooper (barrel maker), a cook, ten to twelve seamen, a handful of landsmen, and one or two ship's boys. The chief mate, second in command, minded security of the vessel, making sure the slaves were under control; regarding hardware, the African slaves were controlled with the use of manacles, shackles, neck rings, chains, cat-o'-nine-tails, speculum oris, and thumbscrews. See Rediker, *Slaveship*, 56–58.

5. Palmer, *Slaves of the White God*, 17.

6. Long, *Ellipsis*, 281.

7. No doubt, as Emma Christopher notes, "a plethora of deities, spirits and ancestors were beseeched for wisdom, strength, and help." Christopher, *Freedom*, 73–74.

was genuinely worth little on board the slave ship. Slave traders, to be sure, were motivated by a desire to obtain wealth via the trade and purchase of their human cargo, so there was a fundamental interest in keeping slaves alive. However, their sinister plan aimed to invest extraordinarily little and gain as much as possible. As would be the case with any merchant vessel conducting business during the transatlantic era, risks and losses were calculated to maximize profit.[8] The African slave trade was no different. It was an insidious business, but it had its methodology, nonetheless.

By 1441, Europeans began systematically pursuing free labor to expand and dominate the new global economy of chattel enslavement. As a pragmatic business maneuver, slave traders often tried to load as much *black gold* onto ships as humanely possible, even if such a move entailed giving up necessary amounts of food and water rations. John Hope Franklin's research reveals, "There are records of ships as small as 90 tons carrying a complement of 390 slaves in addition to crew and provisions."[9] John Thornton, moreover, notes that researchers during the era documented that overloading ships from the sixteenth to the seventeenth century was a common practice among private captains.[10] This experience invariably translated into a torturous existence for the newly enslaved Africans.

Scholars have studied and reflected upon this torturous existence with awe and bewilderment. Because when investigated thoroughly, one is left with utter amazement that a single African survived. Once onboard the slave ship and out of sight of the African shoreline, the reality of this ill-fated experience set deep within the African soul. In *There Is a River*, Vincent Harding posits that newly enslaved Africans "gulped down handfuls of sand in the last effort to hold the reality of the land."[11] As early as the beginning of the twentieth century, W. E. B. Du Bois, in awe, stated, "The rude change in this [black] life was the slave ship."[12] The "unearthly moans

---

8. The psychological association between the trauma of the slave ship, and the religious and moral appellation projected upon the experience of said trauma, led many slave ship survivors to abhor white Christianity once a quasi-comparative analysis was conducted. Slave religion would attempt to restore cosmological order by appropriating Western religion with that of their African traditions of worship. The fact that some slave ships were named *Integrity, Justice, Jesus*, and *Gift of God* illuminates the moral and spiritual depravity of the slave trade. See Harding, *There Is a River*, 3.
9. Franklin and Moss, *From Slavery*, 44.
10. Thornton, *Africa and Africans*, 155.
11. Harding, *There Is a River*, 3.
12. Du Bois, *Souls of Black Folk*, 138.

THE SLAVE SHIP EXPERIENCE

and piercing shrieks," Sterling Stuckey enumerates, "and the smell of the filth and stench of death, all during the violent rhythms and quiet coursings of ships at sea."[13] With concentrated intrigue, Charles Long contends that the slave ship experience demanded that the African spiritual and religious beliefs be put to the ultimate test; in this experience, argues Long, the enslaved African, trapped in this horrific social circumstance, had to form some level of doubt regarding a *power* that could display presence when they needed it the most. Professor Long wonders, "To whom does one pray from the bowels of a slave ship?"[14] Indeed, one must wonder, to whom? This rude change in black life, in Du Boisian language, is further articulated in a response by Mahommah Gardo Baquaqua when he reflects on the time he experienced the *owa coco*, the dreaded slave ship.[15] "When we reached the beach and stood on the sand, oh!" cries Baquaqua, "How I wished that the sand would open and swallow me up. My wretchedness I cannot describe."[16] Cudjo Lewis, the African-born slave who was a captive on board the last recorded slave ship, confided in Zora Neale Hurston that "De boat we on called the *Clotilde*. Cudjo suffers so in dat ship."[17]

The enslaved used the moon's cycles to detect harvest and plant seasons. However, this information did not help them navigate and understand their geographical location or cosmic rhythm in the ocean.[18] Herein lies a momentous experience. The enslaved African, with the ability to understand the surrounding world, was cut off from this part of self and forced to exist in a constant state of suffering with no end in view as the ship swayed violently back and forth. A victim of the slave ship experience speaks on this constant state of suffering by simply stating, "It was a horrible scene." Additionally, some Africans, in their state of physical and mental confinement, became frustrated and killed other enslaved Africans to get enough air. Unfortunately, these types of engagements were common.[19]

---

13. Stuckey, *Slave Culture*, 2.
14. Long, *Ellipsis*, 282.
15. Rediker, *Slaveship*, 1.
16. Law and Lovejoy, *Biography*, 151.
17. Hurston, *Barracoon*, 55.
18. Smallwood, *Saltwater Slavery*, 135.
19. Women slaves were also killed with a degree of barbarity and desperation; for instance, they used their fingernails as weapons and dug them deep into the brains of their shipmates. See E. Taylor, *If We Must Die*, 32.

The eighteenth-century slave ship doctor Alexander Falconbridge noted two elements that fit normalcy for the enslaved aboard slave ships.[20] They are death and sexual assault. Olaudah Equiano, in his painful reflection of the slave ship experience, reveals, "The shrieks of the women, and the groans of the dying, rendered it a scene of horror almost unconceivable . . . and I began to hope that death would soon put an end to my miseries."[21] Equiano further explains the psychological depth of the slave ship experience by unveiling that "one day, when we had a smooth sea and moderate wind, two of my wearied countrymen, who were chained together, preferring death to such a life of misery, somehow made through the nettings and jumped into the sea."[22]

The sexual assaults, including on male slaves and children, would happen onboard the slave ship and continue on various lands in the *New World*, especially in Cuba, under Spanish enslavement. Itanoko, a slave who was raped by his owner, Urban, recollects that it was a "ravishing violation."[23] Moreover, the slave ship doctor noted that sailors did indeed rape vulnerable slaves, mature and immature, and death seemed to be a constant issue; for instance, finding a "dead slave connected to a living slave in the morning" was a regular occurrence.[24] Sexual gratification was such an ideal notion that white men physically assaulted one another to secure first rights to the rape of a good-looking African woman.[25] One slaver named Philippe Liot won first rights and proceeded to cover the mouth of, rape, and molest an eight-to-ten-year-old for three days and three nights. Sadly, the young African girl's attempts to scream were thwarted by his venous hand.[26]

Nevertheless, bonds were formed in this chaotic environment; as a matter of fact, the African slaves aboard slave ships were referred to as shipmates in various locations, such as the Batiments of Haiti, the Malungo of Brazil, the Malongue of Trinidad, and the Mati of Surinam.[27] They would sleep, eat, cry, and eventually learn to fight together. In moments of rebellion, enslaved Africans aboard slave ships worked together and used the

20. Rediker, *Slaveship*, 45, 59.
21. Equiano, "Interesting Narrative," 60.
22. Equiano, "Interesting Narrative," 61.
23. Foster, "Sexual Abuse of Black Men," 125–30.
24. Falconbridge, *Account of the Slave Trade*, 24–28.
25. E. Taylor, *If We Must Die*, 34.
26. E. Taylor, *If We Must Die*, 35.
27. Diouf, *Dreams of Africa*, 68.

world around them, as would be the cultural logic of the times, to create space for a more realistic chance of achieving freedom. The hellish world around them consisted of "swords, sabers, guns, razors, pikes, knives, axes, hammers, files, buckets, scissors, sledgehammers, boiling water, oars, food bowls, chains, bars, and pieces of wood."[28]

If hell truly exists, the slave ship is its most infamous associate. To be sure, the slave ship is essentially where African peoples became identified as a suffering, bonded people—oppression forced this peculiar metamorphosis to occur.[29] One example of this early stage of bondedness is that although language barriers persisted, drum usage was one way enslaved Africans communicated with one another among a sea of many African languages. The slave ship experience, no doubt, caused a cosmic shift for the enslaved Africans and was a vehicle from which this bonded metamorphosis would occur.[30]

Traditionally, the Middle Passage is situated in the Atlantic. There is credence to the argument, however, that the Middle Passage should include the capture, holding, chaining, marching, and imprisonment on the coast within the framework of what is presented as a pivotal point in the enslaved experience of branded black chattel. Michael Gomez is correct when he argues that the Middle Passage was where the enslaver and enslaved vied for the right to define one's purpose and destiny in the *New World*. It is in the slave ship experience, however, that black Africans are forced to bond together beyond the shores of Africa, despite tribal differentiation or where their ancestors dwelled, to fight against white and black oppressors and strive to survive and identify with a bondedness of necessity.

---

28. E. Taylor, *If We Must Die*, 96.

29. I agree with other scholars about the polyvalent nature of African peoples; however, I argue that this cultural norm was disrupted when enslaved Africans were separated from their culturally found ethnic groups and forced to grapple with whether to unite with other enslaved people. Although there were instances in which ethnic groups were self-identified (there is a tendency to associate with that which is familiar), white slavers discovered that *mixing* of ethnic groups would decrease the probability of African communication, thereby subverting the reality of a unified protest and rebellion.

30. I rely a great deal upon the research of Sterling Stuckey about this matter of African bondedness. He rightly says that the "slave ships were the first real incubators of slave unity across cultural lines." Africans from various ethnic backgrounds (e.g., Yorubas, Akans, Ibos, and Angolans) experienced the common horror of the slave ship. For Stuckey, and I tend to agree, this horrific space of physical and psychological trauma produced a *single people*. The commonality shared was that of resistance toward a white domination system. See Stuckey, *Slave Culture*, 1.

THE PROBLEM OF BLACK SKIN

The enslaved Africans who survived the typical three-month trek to the *New World* did so as new black beings—the slave ship experience changed them. This cultural transformation pattern runs from Haiti, Jamaica, Barbados, Antigua, the Bahamas, and the Americas. Yes, the spiritual depth of this cultural pattern has diminished over time; be that as it may, the message is still evident. The slave ship experience should be considered the most definitive moment in black culture. It is a moment of suffering, transformation, struggle, love, sacrifice, courage, and fortitude. It was all of these things and more. Despite the chains, whips, disease, malnutrition, sickness, trauma of dark and tight confinement, and rape, many enslaved Africans nevertheless discovered new elements of community, spiritual depth, ingenuity, cultural identity, and power.[31] To this end, the slave ship experience is a beautiful struggle.

---

31. Taken from their land, many Africans, I presume, grappled with ancestral duty and individual action to help better understand the reality of their suffering. The enslaved religious leader would have been the person to address such a concern.

6

PRESSING FORWARD/ PRESSED BACKWARD

(*The Spirit of Black Progression and Black Privilege*)

From the barracoons to the slave ship to the plantation, class distinction within blackness stretches the collective to the point of causing stagnation in the movement toward black liberation from one generation after another. As a result of black-on-black *othering* becoming a cultural fixture throughout the *New World* enslavement process, I argue essentially that privilege is sometimes abused within black space and presents as a fundamental cause of black stagnation. I also suggest generational growth can only occur when black people are intellectually honest about why they are who they are (i.e., better understand the historical trajectory of a phenomenon). This can only happen when the educational experience matches the spirit and energy of the people. Currently, the spirit of black progression (i.e., *black zeitgeist*), although moving, vibrates and moves at a low frequency due to white oppressive measures, which are also employed by blacks upon the lived experience of other blacks within their sub-world, thus creating, substantiating, and perpetuating social practices of collective stagnation.[1]

---

1. See the analysis of "Perseverance of the Black Spirit," in L. Bennett, *Before the Mayflower*, 411–44.

THE PROBLEM OF BLACK SKIN

MOVEMENT AND INFLUENCE OF THE *BLACK ZEITGEIST*

The essence of black survival and wherewithal is undergirded by individuals who are and were possessed with the *black zeitgeist* in a concentrated effort to further the fight toward ultimate liberation for black people and, by default, set the stage to get world freedom. I presume the term *black zeitgeist* is appropriate when trying to better understand the essence of the black complaint to America. It is the *black zeitgeist*, the ever-moving spirit of the times, that presents the truth about the oppressive experience of black people in every generational cycle. This nuanced expression of what many thinkers and scholars would take as a fragmented understanding of the governing spirit of history is aligned with expressing and experiencing the Christian tradition through the lens of a nuanced Jesus (i.e., black Jesus). As seen in James Cones's *The Cross and the Lynching Tree* and Kelly Brown Douglas's *The Black Christ*, black Jesus is codified in a way that bends closer to the ground-level position of social agony and cultural desperation. As the great Hebrew prophet Ezekiel would assert, "I sat where they sat." Black Jesus sits with black people and becomes one who bears the burden of black-skin affiliation. Jesus indeed desires to be black, is black, because it is in the blackness that one discovers the many contradictions of divine order within the human experience. In Jesus's time, Jews needed a nuanced savior, a Messiah, a person filled with the spirit of divine justice who was ordained to change the lived experience of the Jews who were oppressed under Roman social laws and customs. For many contemporary Jews, the desire and anticipation remain. Why? Because they believe that God wants more for them in this life, and according to God's divine plan, the messiah arrives within the context of generational expansion and human growth.

In a similar vein, the *black zeitgeist* can be seen operating, for instance, in the life of Martin Luther King Jr. He was most certainly considered a savior for black people. He was killed, like Jesus, because of his demand for social liberation for specific people and the world in general. It must be understood that the *black zeitgeist* can also take possession of the white body, mind, and soul, and be used to address social oppression. Although fraught with many biases about the nature of blackness, the nineteenth-century abolition movement is an example of the *black zeitgeist* moving the cause for black social liberation, strangely enough, via white skin. John Brown, taking up a plan to free the enslaved via direct action of violence and being possessed to the point of frustration by the inaction of several black leaders, took some of the weight of black cultural oppression upon his shoulders and sparked what some consider to be the first salvo in the American Civil War in 1859, a couple of years earlier than the consensus of an 1861 date.[2] Indeed, John Brown, in a sense, was the spark that fueled the violent war between the North and South. Eventually Abraham Lincoln, the legislative architect of emancipation and advocate of black migration outside of the United States, agreed with his conscience and reasoned that it was justifiably expedient to contextually free enslaved African Americans. However, the assassination of President Lincoln thwarted the potential trajectory of newly freed black people in America, thus crushing the desired outcome that John Brown and many others who became owned by the *black zeitgeist* had desperately envisioned.

SOCIAL STRATIFICATION AND BLACK PRIVILEGE

Black privilege entails having the power to manipulate space, regardless of the degree, within the black sub-world. Black privilege, however, can also be used within white space (whenever allowed to do so) to progress and/or regress black space. This is a powerful phenomenon as it entices one to the possibility of more, and more is often found within the confines of white space. An apt example would be blacks who are first and second generations removed from the experience of chattel enslavement; nevertheless, they struggle to find social spacing within the Jim Crow–era because of closed opportunities within white space and a desire to prove a level of significance and worth, consciously and unconsciously, by mirroring social formations of so-called civilized white society.

In the early twentieth century, abbreviated survival tactics were employed within the black sub-world. These survival tactics are also visible in how black college students attending white universities appropriated a Eurocentric way of surviving by founding fraternities and sororities that privileged members in a similar vein to the white college experience. "Emblematic of the paradox of double-consciousness," as scholars suggest, "BLGOs reveal the contradictions of the black quest for elite status in the

---

2. It is suggested that at the beginning of the Civil War, one would be hard pressed to find one white in a hundred who believed black people could integrate freely into a democratically perceived American race-based society. See Du Bois, *Black Reconstruction*, 191.

midst of group oppression."[3] This experience would manifest in a morbid understanding of sub-stratification elitism. Eugene Robinson, for instance, shows four subgroups that help illustrate this mode of existence in the black sub-world.[4]

Black students had created a space of access to social organizations that catered to an African American cultural ethos, which proved invaluable as it provided a sense of togetherness in a world that negated the worth of black human personality. However, black social organizations soon began to deny this privileged space to individuals who looked like them and who potentially met with the same social injustices. This experience is reminiscent of the plantation ethos in which a minority of blacks discovered comfort in the replication of a white world within a black sub-world. It provided a sense of significance and control to people denied the experience of full-fledged freedom. "While all of the slaves were always under the surveillance of the whites," according to E. Franklin Frazier, "the house servants constantly lived in close association with their masters. These house servants have often been associated with their masters since childhood. Consequently, they early got the speech of their masters, a fact which set them off from the more isolated field hands, who spoke a dialect."[5] Frazier finds this type of idealism in what I refer to as *early slave submission politics*. He further asserts, "Generally, the son of a house servant was apprenticed to some artisan to learn a skilled trade. These skilled mechanics, who constituted a large section of the artisans in the South, formed a sort of privileged class in the slave community with house servants."[6]

The notion of the abuse of privilege and active engagement of racist tendencies among blacks is met with extreme criticism within some pockets of the sub-world. The compromising intellectual, for instance, argues such a phenomenon away by suggesting that blacks do not have enough power and resources to erect and sustain a social world in which blacks can *systematically* limit access and dominate other racial groups. But this

---

3. Washington and Nuñez, "Education, Racial Uplift," 171. It is also important to note that Gloria Harper Dickinson presents an uncanny nexus between West African initiation ceremonies and that of the early twentieth-century Black Greek Letter Organization pledge practices and rituals. See Dickinson, "Pledged to Remember."

4. Mainstream middle-class majority (Americanized); abandoned minority with little hope of social improvement; small transcendent elite with enormous wealth; mixed race and black immigrants. See Robinson, *Disintegration*, 5.

5. Frazier, *Black Bourgeoisie*, 12.

6. Frazier, *Black Bourgeoisie*, 13.

argument is a deflection from the fact that social stratification creates spaces of fractural oppression even within segments of oppressed groups. Consider, for instance, incarcerated individuals and their ability to set up a social hierarchy of privilege even though they are oppressed. Incarcerated individuals can create and operate within their constructed sub-world to maintain a semblance of power and control over their environments. Prisons are known to run on terms of inmate law; the officers and guards are merely there to maintain a degree of order. But to be clear, inmate politics dictate who receives certain privileges. In a similar vein, blacks, under the social scope of oppression within the white world, nevertheless create meaning and purpose within a funneled-down sub-world in which power and privilege are used to dominate oppressed black space while also craving a degree of privilege within white space. Moreover, it is often argued that black people cannot be racist based on similar analyses about power, social positioning, and lack of privilege. I disagree with such notions.

In 1959, Mike Wallace and Louis Lomax produced a documentary titled *The Hate That Hate Produced*. This work focused on the rise of Black nationalism and the Nation of Islam. This production would be the first introduction of Malcolm X onto the national stage as a radical leader. The controversial title inferred that the hate of black skin also produced the hate of white skin. This is an accurate presupposition. When I saw George Floyd Jr.'s murder, I looked at all white people as if they placed a knee on Floyd's neck. Their skin affiliation was the cultural trigger that fired off my correlation to black pain and suffering with that of white skin; in that space of emotional unrest, all people with white skin were suspect. I was living in the proverbial space of *The Hate That Hate Produced*. Regardless of goodwill and intentionality toward black people, if a person had white skin, I subconsciously categorized such a person along the same thread as former police officer Derek Chauvin. By delving into a deep self-analysis, I learned that *I hated* someone based on their skin affiliation. This is unhealthy and most deleterious. If I were to prejudge a person negatively based on race affiliation, I would certainly consider myself a racist, regardless of the form of justification.

No form of hate, even if justified on a retaliatory basis, should be embraced as it influences the moral decline of the bearer. This is not to argue that blacks, in particular, should become passive and submissive in their relationship to oppression. Black people should protect themselves, in the spirit of Malcolm X, *by any means necessary*. Such protection, however, should be done with clarity of heart and mind. I have learned to attempt to carry love in my heart for everyone, even adversaries. Still, when the time arises to fight, and there are no alternatives beyond the prospect of being harmed, one must engage with focus, power, and an unrelenting spirit of bravery rather than hate. Perhaps some would refer to such a phenomenon as an experience of tempered righteous indignation.

It should be noted that black racism is different from white racism in terms of power and authority. For instance, there is a long memory in which the legal system has worked in concert with cultural and societal thinking on black skin. Therefore, black people have learned to withhold potentially ill-conceived and ill-timed reactions to what they consider the all-consuming *white gaze* of retaliation. This is an act of survival; of course, there have always been exceptions to this rule. But most black people are taught both consciously and unconsciously to withhold an essence of self when in white presence.

White people, on the other hand, have the freedom and privilege to react to their emotions and feelings about blackness without the burden of wondering what would happen to them. This is certainly true during the lynching era in which black men, women, and children became, in the words of Billie Holiday, "strange fruit," by speaking what is on their minds.[7] Black people do not have the privilege to talk with ease within white space. The slightest infraction could send them into the social abyss of blackness, being situated further from the exposure of potential rations of whiteness. Black survival in white space is based on one's ability to *code switch*. However, black people can react in the fullness of their essence when occupying black space. It is here where one sees abuse occur more clearly.

The murder of Tyre Nichols in 2023 by five black officers in Memphis is an apt example of how privileged blacks have the ability, due to black-skin affiliation, to oppress others within the same black sub-world and create dysfunctional experiences in which their angst of social limitation is projected upon someone who looks like them. I contend that these five black men would not have conducted themselves in such an evil manner had Tyre been a white man. The five police officers had the privilege of stopping Tyre. They pulled him out of his vehicle in the spirit of civic duty and concern and began taking turns beating him to death while using policing

---

7. Holiday, "Strange Fruit." There were at least four thousand documented black victims of lynching between 1877 and 1950. The lynching method consisted of hangings, burnings, shootings, drownings, stabbings, and beatings. See Equal Justice Initiative, *Lynching in America*.

language such as "stop resisting." Thus, this experience is undoubtedly an abuse of black power and privilege. I imagine Tyre Nichols learned to negotiate the terrain of the white world with relative success, only to be killed by people with whom he may have presumed he had a cultural bond. How can there be movement toward liberation when black people in positions of power choose to abuse people who look like them? This question must be raised, and it must be answered with rigor. This goal is achievable through systematic study of the concept of black privilege.

BLACK PRIVILEGE STUDIES (*AN ORIENTATION*)

My notion of *black privilege*, which is briefly highlighted in *Existential Togetherness* (2019), entails the belief that investment and trade practitioners among African elites and slave-rendering service technicians among the African working class instituted a phenomenon that would, on the one hand, create chaos in terms of Africans often times being kidnapped, branded, stored on the shore, and finally placed in the dreaded slave ship and shipped to various locations in the *New World*. Families were torn apart and communities were left in shambles. On the other hand, amid this chaotic experience, something else emerged.

As various Africans found themselves chained to other enslaved Africans from multiple regions, bonds were formed. A collective of uncompromising enslaved Africans, despite the inability to understand one another's native tongue at times, pulled on common African themes and cultural experiences and created a newly developing black human being motivated and inspired to be free once again, even if such motivations and inspirations led to a violent death. To be sure, some Africans, whether seizing the opportunity to profit from the business of black bodies or seizing the opportunity to obtain freedom from enslavement at the expense of other black bodies, became compromising blacks, uncoalesced hybrid blacks, as it were.

From the outset of the *New World* experience, black people have had to deal with issues of betrayal from other black people. This experience is ingrained in the black psyche. Contemporary blacks will undoubtedly discover, if investigated honestly, that black-on-black *othering* happens by way of an unconscious reaction for many. A rationalist perhaps would counter this point by suggesting that all cultural groups deal with issues that may cause, at times, discord and dysfunctional actions. But I challenge such a refutation on the basis that enslavement, Jim Crow, and the current American societal apparatus provide evidence that should inspire blacks with the shared lived experience of oppression to consider the significance of togetherness. If indeed chattel slavery, Jim Crow, and modern-day racism are as terrible as believed within black space, why is there still no mass movement afoot?

In response, Eric Taylor's *If We Must Die* posits that black scholars who study the history of slavery and Jim Crow have a tendency to "imagine an idealized version of the past."[8] However, Taylor agrees that enslaved Africans banded together and fought for freedom in many instances. Still, he reasons the notion of a unified slave consciousness is nevertheless a fallacy. Additionally, Taylor comes to this conclusion because of how some enslaved Africans internalized bondage. Some felt they deserved it, while others were afraid or set on betrayal and became antithetical to any notion of togetherness. To this end, Taylor is correct in that some enslaved Africans were afraid or sought the first opportunity to align with thoughts and actions of betrayal. I disagree, however, with the conclusion of his analysis.

To be clear, Taylor's negation of a unified slave consciousness is based on the reasoning that some Africans aboard slave ships would have come to a point in their suffering in which they blamed themselves for their enslavement. Some sat and watched while other enslaved Africans fought and died. Some took African rebellion as a chance to garner sympathy and perhaps even freedom by compromising plots of rebellion with betrayal.[9] What makes Taylor's analysis problematic is the presumption that unified slave consciousness should possibly entail 100-percent, or a majority of, commitment from those enslaved Africans occupying the same geographically oppressive space.

Let us also presume that the former statement exaggerates a fact and that Taylor believes the percentage should be closer to 50 to 75. Would this range suffice and fulfill the requirements of a unified slave consciousness designation? If two enslaved Africans out of one hundred or one thousand on board a slave ship endured the ebb and flow of the sea, language barriers, rape, malnutrition, fights with fellow slaves, and both physical and mental trauma, the requirement for a unified slave consciousness has been fulfilled. The initial Africans who had the burden of being the first wave of rebellious slaves would have experienced a sense of existential togetherness

---

8. E. Taylor, *If We Must Die*, 106.
9. E. Taylor, *If We Must Die*, 6–7.

by way of being chained to another enslaved African and not being able to understand another's native tongue. If they could agree to perhaps do away with any past grievances one African may have had with other cultures and ethnic groups of other Africans, unity was established, trust embraced, and both enslaved Africans moved toward the end result of liberation and freedom.

The *black zeitgeist* occupied this new form of black bondedness and inspired wave after wave of African rebellion from what we can currently study from 1509 to 1865 documents. Interestingly enough, Taylor's research shows just how fluid of an impression the *black zeitgeist* has on the African enslaved populace onboard the slave ship. For instance, out of 493 boats that are documented as being vessels in which enslaved Africans rebelled, 100,000 enslaved Africans could have born witness to ship insurrections; out of this number, Taylor argues that 75,000 or more of these slaves would have made it to the shores of the Americas and various other lands in the *New World*. The tales of blood, gore, heroes, heroines, and betrayal would have been seared into the consciousness of these enslaved Africans.

These stories of valor would not be suppressed; instead, they would have been shared orally with a warning to future generations that they, too, are obligated to fight. Although the same black spirit of progression that formed when chains bonded two differentiated Africans together in an experience of desperation and despair and helped many other enslaved Africans find the courage to fight against enslavement over several centuries, the current plight of black people globally and in America, in particular, suggests however that the pressure from both white and black spaces upon black people is somehow hindering more significant strides from being achieved.

In *It's Time to Talk About "Black Privilege"* John Blake asserts that David Horowitz's *Black Skin Privilege and the American Dream* is one example of how whites attempt to deflect from the reality of their unearned space in the world by countering with notions such as the absurdity of blacks having privilege, too. Horowitz, as Blake writes, notes that the idea of *black privilege* (i.e., that blacks have systemic advantages) can be traced to an 1883 Supreme Court decision in which Justice Joseph Bradley presented as the majority opinion that laws placed too much emphasis on black accommodation. Blake also notes that the mention of *black privilege* within academic circles invariably entails laughter and scoffing, particularly from noted white privilege scholar Peggy McIntosh, who believes that whites who espouse notions of black advantage do so as a ploy to deflect from the reality of bequeathed privilege within *whiteness*. Parishioners of *whiteness* are merely pawns acting to a particular end. The systemic structure they protect is the issue that must be grappled with, a fact that Horowitz does not acknowledge in his thesis. His use of the 1883 Supreme Court decision as a basis of his argument for black privilege is an experience a person with white skin has the comfort of enjoying. If explained correctly, I imagine most black people could see how the 1883 Supreme Court decision affected the trajectory of contemporary black oppression. Just a couple of decades removed from a centuries-old practice of chattel enslavement, the High Court (an intricate part of the American domination system) refused to privilege enslaved blacks with equal opportunity in society.

Interestingly enough, talk host personality Charlamagne Tha God's *Black Privilege* is a treatise on how Charlamagne obtained a certain level of success by living his true authentic self. He acknowledges that everyone has privileges. "No matter what sort of struggles you've faced," Charlamagne contends, "you still have a unique privilege. Do you have arms and legs? That is good. Well, then, you have limb privilege. You have an advantage over the Iraqi vet who lost his and is trying to learn how to walk on bionic legs."[10] He alludes to the employment of universal privilege, which promotes a sense of existential responsibility to create and define purposeful meaning despite everyday circumstances. Charlamagne's work speaks to the ingenious heritage of oppressed blacks by asserting that grit, opportunity, and sacrifice remove any excuse for failure within the American domination system. Although his narrative is inspirational, the reality is still that there are blacks who have grit but will never be exposed to specific opportunities based on systemic racial discrimination. As a result of his success, however, Charlamagne got a certain degree of privilege in both black and white spaces. However, for black people to gain more privileged space, more blacks must continue to use their privilege for good by creating more positive black space for others who look like them.

Cassi Pittman Claytor's *Black Privilege: Modern Middle-Class Blacks with Credentials and Cash to Spend* highlights the New York cultural terrain in which elite blacks balance the worlds of capital means, white social engagement, and black cultural reliance. This work is a beautiful elemental analysis of the problem of black negotiation with wealth between white and black space within a specific geographical location. Additionally, Eugene

---

10. Charlamagne Tha God, *Black Privilege*, 281. See also Blake, "It's Time to Talk."

Robinson's *Disintegration: The Splintering of Black America*, E. Franklin Frazier's *Black Bourgeoisie,* Lawrence Otis Graham's *Our Kind of People,* Shomari Wills's *Black Fortunes,* Ellis Cose's *The Rage of a Privileged Class: Why Are Middle-Class Blacks Angry? Why Should America Care?* Harold Cruse's *The Crisis of the Negro Intellectual* and Elizabeth Dowling Taylor's *The Original Black Elite* certainly add substance to the fact that black people have benefited economically and socially within a newly constructed sub-world; but one must ask, how are such wealth and privilege being utilized to further enhance the whole of black life?

7

THE LEGITIMATION OF WHITENESS

(The Du Boisian Entanglement of Religion, Morality, and Society)[1]

The notion of Whiteness is a mental construct that is legalistically embedded in cultural norms, with law and religion providing foundational support through consistent instruction. The psychology and philosophy of whiteness that W. E. B. Du Bois outlines in the early twentieth century are also present in what many would call twenty-first-century systemic racism. With a gifted mind and lived experience within the *veil*, Du Bois placed innumerable values upon the essence of the black social world and its associated *otherness*. Such a world consists of many variations of experiences.

To alleviate some toil associated with unpacking such a complex experience of blackness, Du Bois aggressively investigates the problem of race and finds it to be tethered to the nature of every black individual residing in the world. Still, it is America where he focuses his interrogative gaze.

---

1. How people conceptualize and interpret God creates a distinct social world in which moral ideas influence human behavior. Morality is typically viewed as the highest value of what is suitable for an individual within a given society. See Otto, *Idea of the Holy*, 5. A collection of these individualistic thoughts (i.e., morals) forms a collective understanding (i.e., individuals) of what is right and proper for the group (i.e., society). See also Einstein, *World*. As a social construct, religion sets up and reinforces these social norms for the perceived survival and progression of the group. And to go against a religiously legitimated society "is to make a compact with the primeval forces of darkness." Berger, *Sacred Canopy*, 39.

He concludes that American society entails three preeminent phenomena: moral code(s), individual(s), and religious tendencies. All paradoxically share in the structure and maintenance of a society where racism exists.

However, religion carries the most weight for Du Bois because it substantiates normative ideals and morally aligns with how people perceive God, themselves, and others. Therefore, religion's function is to show perennial normalcy of thought and moral behavior within a group of individuals in each society. This essay reflects Du Bois's conflictual and intimate association with both distorting and crossing over the boundary of whiteness and his unique ability to examine facets of religious overtures in legalistic moral behavior within a society he refers to as the *Religion of Whiteness*.

THE *MIXTURE*

A foundational part of legalistic dogma, or human law, is the notion that human beings need structure and guidance to maintain a particular way of existing as a cohesive and expanding social group. Biblical law, for instance, was organized and classified into two groups of interpretation: apodictic laws and casuistic laws. The former merely provides imperatives (i.e., what one ought, expected, and commanded to do). The latter provides a reactionary formula (i.e., how to respond when an act has occurred). In its protasis and apodosis development, casuistic laws became the dominant way to organize social order in the ancient Near East.

Moreover, the casuistic legal paradigm is seen in Exod 21:28–32, 35–36, and early second BCE writings as displayed in the Laws of Eshnunna and the Laws of Hammurabi. In the ancient world, overlords, or kings, who conquered inwardly and then outwardly to peripheral sectors, carried out the organization of groups and thus obtained a basis of legitimate power. Laws were agreements between a governor (i.e., king, overlord, suzerain) and the governed (i.e., underprivileged and/or vassal).

Legalism, in its truest sense, is a social practice in which norms help govern and guide how one reflects primarily and how one ought to behave to nurture strict ideals, with legitimacy, upon the surrounding world. Moral law, a contributing factor to legalism, derives from a religious understanding of how God, self, and others are structured and codified in a social setting. Within governed social groups, there is also a tendency for sub-privileged individuals to appear and carve more privileged space for themselves while depressing further still the marginalized of the sub-world.

Such a phenomenon is seen aptly in the Second Temple priesthood. Although the priesthood could not carve power and position from the empire, according to Herbert Marbury, "It could legislate local policies and appropriate symbolic resources, such as its ability to effect normative constructs of ethnic identity and gender roles, to control as much as possible the flow of material resources within the community."[2]

Legalism has also been a gift and a curse as an ethical code and compass (i.e., legitimizing proper and improper notions of human behavior) to the Christian church in America. On the one hand, for instance, a bent toward religious moralism helped shape the justification for the legalization of racism, which is based solely on a belief that God designed racial hierarchy to privilege one group over another; on the other hand, religious moralism helped shape the justification for delegitimizing the legalization of racism and American chattel enslavement of blacks via protest and, sometimes, violent means. What does this dialectical dilemma entail? Let us, then, reflect more deeply upon religion's purpose and how it serves as a moral guidepost in society.[3]

Because of the paradoxical element of religion (i.e., the morals of the individuals), a world of social substantiation is created, entailing an illicit way of being and existing in the surrounding world among various peoples and other opposing supernatural powers. To this end, as Sigmund Freud suggested years ago, religion is constructed to provide meaning and a code of existence for a particular group of people. That civilization itself is built upon the doctrines of religion.[4] "Every human society," according

---

2. See Kant, *Foundations*, 29–31; Holtz, "Reading Biblical Law"; Habermas, *Legitimation*, 36–37; Marbury, *Imperial Dominion*, 88.

3. Abraham Joshua Heschel's contention that "human existence cannot derive its ultimate meaning from society, because society itself is in need of meaning" provides a framework for introducing the paradoxical problem of disentangling religion, individual(s), and moral(s). My contention is that society, which forms individuals, sets the moral standards for which people in said society should govern themselves. Heschel's main point is that God is the source of societal organization. But this view becomes problematic when one considers the fact that God is also a human construction, ideally. See Heschel, *Man*, 196. Nicolas Berdyaev uses the phraseology *religious fanaticism* to describe how human ideas can become fundamentally processed at extreme levels; whereby "the idea of God, of moral perfection, of justice, freedom, love, knowledge. When this happens, the living God, the living perfection, the actual justice, love, freedom and knowledge disappear, since everything living, and concrete can only exist in the full and harmonious correlation of parts in a whole. Every value turns into an idol and becomes a lie and a deception." Berdyaev, *Destiny*, 171.

4. Freud, *Future*, 44.

THE LEGITIMATION OF WHITENESS

to Peter Berger, "is an enterprise of world-building. Religion occupies a unique place in this enterprise." Berger also believes religion has been the "effective instrumentality of legitimation throughout history. All legitimation supports a socially defined reality. Religion legitimates so effectively because it relates the precarious reality constructions of empirical societies with ultimate reality."[5]

Furthermore, religion influences morality as it pertains to understanding how a group of individuals collectively arrives at a consensus of differentiating good and evil, right and wrong. It is an experience in which the sacred intersects with the profane, and a coming of terms occurs through verbal and nonverbal agreement regarding relational duties between existing parties.[6] To be sure, all human beings worship something.[7]

Humans produce religion, which informs how they respond to God, self, and others. Such a process leads to uncertainty about the guidelines defining good and evil. Parishioners of the *religion of whiteness* are immoral when they continue to exist in a society where they are uplifted and black people are continually downtrodden. This must be remedied. Unfortunately, the remedy exists in the individual(s), so attacking institutions, as Du Bois concluded, will prove only futile without understanding the phenomenon's interrelatedness.

Sometimes, the good from one religious legitimation can be experienced as bad for another. For example, the enslavement of African people was justified within a Christian orthodox tradition. For white Christians in the *New World*, God would use the enlightened Christian world to mentor the presumedly less civilized Africans in the ways of proper moral behavior. On the other hand, the newly enslaved Africans, with a dense history in spiritual and religious study and practice, called upon supernatural powers

---

5. Berger, *Sacred Canopy*, 32.

6. Friedrich Schleiermacher believed that study of religion illuminated one's conception and understanding of the universe; in all its complexities, the universe, as Schleiermacher fashioned, was an ideal comparison to the nature of how human cosmic realities intersect, collide, and explode into a new organized existence of *chaotic* structure. See Schleiermacher, *On Religion*, 24.

7. According to Erich Fromm, "there is" not nor will there ever be "one without a religious need, a need to have a frame of orientation and an object of devotion . . . man may worship animals, trees, idols of gold or stone, an invisible god, a saintly man or diabolic leaders; he may worship his ancestors, his nation, his class or party, money or success; his religion may be conducive to the development of destructiveness or of love, of domination or of brotherliness; it may further his power of reason or paralyze it." Fromm, *Psychoanalysis*, 25–26.

in their moments of captivity and engaged in what they considered the justifiable killings of their captives. European slavers had a clear understanding of the dangers associated with attempting to enslave Africans. Still, it was a risk they were willing to take because the reward was so great. They felt obligated based on the religious mandate from the divine regarding their destiny of European supremacy (i.e., whiteness). This religious practice gave birth to the societal problem of black skin.

THE INTERSECTION OF RELIGION, WHITENESS, AND BLACK-SKIN *OTHERNESS*

Du Bois set out on a quest to understand why black people suffered so immensely in a nation that professes to be the world's moral standard. The attention that white people placed on white as great and black as inept was fascinating and appalling to Du Bois. On the one hand, he was fascinated by white supremacy's intricate ways and religious patterns of development. On the other hand, he was appalled at the type of hypocrisy displayed within the context of moral reasoning. Moreover, the *religion of whiteness* was so deeply aged and embedded in American culture that it was near impossible to convince a parishioner that they were wrong. To be sure, the Duboisian ambition was to get parishioners of the religion of whiteness to denounce their faith and compromise their morals.

To address the natural entanglement of bad morals, religious bias, and dubious societal norms effectively, Mark C. Taylor suggests that *denaturing* has to occur to move beyond what has come to be considered a cultural standard.[8] Societies exist when people join and develop a social contract, written or oral, but clearly defined by rules and a distinct moral understanding, which entails existential consequences for violating the consensual norm.[9] This phenomenon is most aptly seen, for example, in the 1950s and 1960s social experience when the integrationist northerners attempted to change a southern society's criteria and constructs, which was highly

---

8. M. Taylor, *About Religion*, 80.

9. For African Americans, Peter Paris argues that the primary ethical concern is that of developing a "moral character that reflects the basic values of their respective communities. Morality pertains to the cultural ethos and hence is culturally specific. According to this perspective, there is no universal morality as such, even though some common moral values are widespread among diverse cultural groups." Paris, *Virtues and Values*, 13.

determined to maintain its segregationist existence. People come into conflict when boundaries are crossed and *existing ways* are challenged.[10]

Maria Stewart, the first black woman to publish thoughts about America's moral and political hypocrisy, implores, "Never will virtue, knowledge, and true politeness begin to flow, till the pure principles of religion and morality are put into force."[11] Like Du Bois, Stewart had the intellectual wherewithal to grapple with the entanglement of religion, morality, and society in America. She was aware that America's moral trajectory began in the 1600s when the institution of slavery became sanctioned as legal under the law.[12] America's highest aim to excel morally was nothing more than a concentrated effort to advance an agenda on how to be better white Christians as outlined in the divine mandate of *manifest destiny*, which meant political and social domination of the world. America did not have an interest in constructing a model and practice of morality that entailed the ethical consideration of blacks; instead, America's interest was centered on how best to exploit, dominate, and control the moral trajectory of the *religion of whiteness*.

The *religion of whiteness*, as Du Bois would argue, continually produced historical inaccuracies about the matter of superior and inferior races. In particular, the European domination system constructed a historical narrative that aligned whiteness with divine positioning and blackness as a sacred instrument used for the sole purpose of white elevation in the world. The calculated and measured construction of slave culture aided in reinforcing a white ideology of dominance and black human negation (i.e., *otherness*) by affording slave masters the legal privilege to flog, rape, lynch, steal, and sell black people. "The absence of recognition," as bell hooks notes, "facilitates making a group the Other."[13] This reality of *otherness* is a psychohistorical construction that distorts human personality and

---

10. In the earliest experience of group interaction, the idea of expansion of land and territory created serious conflict, which led to defining boundaries while also simultaneously distorting and crossing them. However, crossing boundaries was dangerous, so traversing peoples garnered strength by psychologically creating a supernatural force, an image, which would protect them from other supernatural and natural forces existing in the great *beyond*. See Albanese, *America*, 3–5; Horowitz, *Ethnic Groups in Conflict*, 64–74.

11. Stewart, *Maria W. Stewart*, 30.

12. Berry, *Black Resistance*, 2.

13. hooks, "Representing Whiteness," 29.

reconfigures it to subscribe to notions of nothingness and subservience. The former phenomenon is manifested in a philosophically systemic manner.

When analyzing the social maladies of the cultural inner group, black people, and the racial outer group, other peoples of the world, Frantz Fanon concluded that the primary issue underlining many injustices in the world stems from the rather complex and convoluted factors of power, race categorization, and psychological conditioning.[14] To have black skin in the world, according to Fanon, regardless of the geographical point of departure, bears the cultural burden of being labeled by powerful entities and conditioned to live as *other*; moreover, black people, by default, become recipients of a hereditary fate to exist and survive in a world bereft of social inequality, and many under the influence of this lived experience learn to acquiesce and accept notions of tokenism as a measure of personal elevation, familial investment, or operate as a model example for the advancement of the whole of black society.

Othering, in clear terms, is nothing more than a method of negatively distinguishing white from black, not merely on the matter of racial uniqueness but on a higher analytical scale of race being a matter of differentiation of species. Lewis Gordon sums it up in this manner, "But France is not Fanon's Other; he is Frances's Other. Like the African American, Fanon finds himself inextricably linked to a society that rejects him and attempts to deny his existence as a legitimate point of view."[15] This species differentiation of *other*, a denial of humanity, was manifested in the European treatise *The Chronicle of the Discovery and Conquest of Guinea* in 1453. By 1516, Bartolomé de las Casas was lobbying to exchange Taíno natives for Africans. Although he would later in life regret his decision to label black

---

14. "Looking at the immediacies of the colonial context, it is clear," Fanon states emphatically, "that what divides this world is first and foremost what species, what race one belongs to." Fanon, *Wretched of the Earth*, 5. Moreover, an apt example of systemic race differentiation is seen in Jamaican slave culture. For instance, "They divided the offspring of white and black and intermediate shades into 128 divisions. The true Mulatto was the child of the pure black and pure white. The child of the white and 32 parts black. But the quarteron with 96 parts white and 32 parts black. But the quarteron could be produced by the white and the sacatra, in the proportion of 72 to 56 and so on all through the 128 varieties. But the sang-mele with 127 white parts and 1 part was still a man of colour. The Black slaves and Mulattoes hated each other." James, *Jacobins*, 38.

15. Gordon, *Fanon*, 6.

skin as *other*,¹⁶ he set into motion a cultural bell that could not be so quickly silenced.¹⁷

The clarion call educated the *New World* on engaging and responding to black skin. Before this historical pivot, however, as David M. Goldenberg highlights, black skin, even in biblical literature, for instance, was presented in iconography in positive images such as being "militarily powerful, tall, and good looking."¹⁸ By the seventh century, as Muslims began conquering African lands, justification began to develop on a religious basis that the curse of Ham was a valid reason to name Africans as *black* people, thus setting up the cultural reasoning for the enslavement of all African peoples. This type of cultural justification, by the sixteenth century, had set a sturdy foundation upon which both Arab and English would come to differentiate black skin as an ethnic marker of *other*.¹⁹ This happened because of the initial desire for European and opportunistic African excess. David Graeber and David Wengrow would put such an experience of excess in these words:

> We are creatures of excess, and this is what makes us simultaneously the most creative and destructive of all species. . . . Ruling classes are simply those who have organized society in such a way that they can extract the lion's share of that surplus for themselves, whether through tribute, slavery, feudal dues, or manipulating ostensibly free-market arrangements.²⁰

Upon a careful reflection of why the world engaged in war, Du Bois surmised that European avarice was most certainly the cause; furthermore, the United States was hypocritical to presume moral license to police world affairs concerning justice and issues of crimes against humanity.²¹ "No na-

---

16. According to Tudor Parfitt, *Travels of Sir John Mandeville* from 1350–1600 was the foremost authoritative text on global travel and exploration. The work was translated in "German, Dutch, French, English, Latin, Old Irish, Danish, Czech, Spanish, Italian, and other languages." See Parfitt, *Black Jews*, 18.

17. See Kendi, *Stamped*, 23, 26.

18. Goldenberg, *Curse of Ham*, 195.

19. Goldenberg, *Curse of Ham*, 197.

20. Graeber and Wengrow, *Dawn of Everything*, 128.

21. I utilize George Washington Williams's phraseology that he used in a pamphlet entitled *An Open Letter to His Serene Majesty Leopold II, King of the Belgians and Sovereign of the Independent State of Congo*; published in 1890, this treatise outlined ten weighty objections to Leopold II and his attitude and behavior toward the people of the Congo. Franklin, *George*, 243–54.

tion," exhorted Du Bois, "is less fitted for this role."[22] America's presentation and portrayal as a great moral nation contending with evil forces in the world provoked a sense of dismay within Du Bois. Although taken aback, Du Bois understands that reality's cultural ideals are inserted systematically into societal outlets that help normalize behaviors and functioning. "Are we not coming more and more, day by day," he ponders, "to making the statement 'I am white,' the one fundamental tenet of our practical morality."[23]

One would presuppose that the divine notions of justice and equality would set diverse peoples, traditions, and experiences on par with one seamless thought flowing from God's celestial river of inspiration and unequivocal acceptance—this is certainly not the case. Racism, substantiated by notions of *divine favor*, became the *modus operandi* on both conscious and unconscious levels for white people, who faithfully adhered to the code, cultus, creed, and community of sacred ordination of racial inheritance (i.e., the alterity of *blackness* and the centered positing of *whiteness* as a de facto privilege of greatness). To this end, one must focus on how *whiteness* is presented as a bona fide religion.[24]

Whiteness, as Du Bois coined it in the early twentieth century, is a lived experience bereft with racist ideologies, codes, practices, and indoctrination. A logical thread flows from Du Bois's understanding of white people, religion, and moral philosophical formation. One is justified in pondering: Why did he describe a psychological framework of most white people as being faithful worshipers of hatred toward black people? American racism is systematically intentional. Du Bois argues, "She trains her immigrants," for example, "to this despising of 'niggers' from the day of their landing, and they carry and send the news back to the submerged classes in the fatherlands."[25] Racism must be practiced and reinforced socially, or it risks losing generational traction. Eric Fromm pondered this correlation years ago by suggesting one reflect upon social systems such as fascism or Stalinism to bear what Du Bois presented early in the twentieth century: racism has a religious part.[26]

Du Bois's phraseology of *whiteness* is no doubt significant. He used the *religion of whiteness* to frame a description of the depth, organization,

---

22. Du Bois, *Dark Water*, 28.
23. Du Bois, *Dark Water*, 20.
24. See Albanese, *America*, 7.
25. Albanese, *America*, 7.
26. Fromm, *Psychoanalysis*, 32.

emotional, and cultural attachment to an idea or ideology that whites hold as a fundamental tenet of their existence. Du Bois's "The Souls of White Folk" describes the essence of what it means to be white and how the essential basis for the *religion of whiteness* is flawed in conception and scope; nevertheless, it is a reinforced belief that has proven a formidable challenge to the advancement of both whites and blacks. Du Bois viewed racism (caste) as a religious experience devoted to keeping white dominance over the world's people.

In "The Souls of White Folk,"[27] he comes to this fascinating conclusion by first metaphorically lifting himself above the average and naïve thinker and situating himself "high in the tower, where I sit above the loud complaining of the human sea, I know many souls that toss and whirl and pass, but none there are that intrigue me more than the Souls of White folk."[28] Devoid of any ambiguity, Du Bois begins to assert his unique and privileged understanding of the white world. An educated PhD from Harvard, he was a sort of cultural attaché who had learned the foreign land's norms and customs so well that he believed himself to be their equal, not merely a vetted representative of black and white cultural assimilation. Du Bois wrote "The Souls of White Folk" to illuminate and expose the inner workings of what many blacks within the *veil* could not see and proclaim to those whites outside of the *veil* that he was aware of their human ineptness, notwithstanding their established boundaries of race hatred and supremacy; such presentations were rather unimpressive to the scholar, for the depth of his knowledge was such that he contextually understood the essence behind white pretentiousness and bravado.

---

27. "The Souls of White Folk" was originally published in the summer of 1910 in the *Independent*. It was later published in 1920 in Du Bois's autobiography *Dark Water: Voices from Within the Veil*. "The Souls of White Folk," asserts David Levering Lewis, is a type of concluding piece to *The Souls of Black Folk* (1903); in companionship, both works attest to the psychological, religious, historical, and cultural significance of racial construction. *The Souls of Black Folk* spoke to the genius, humanity, and struggle of black people in America. According to Vincent L. Wimbush, "A great part of the purpose of the *Souls* was to celebrate the social power and social gifts and contributions of the people forced behind the veil. The way of doing this was through emphasis placed upon the forms of black expressivity—music, literature, religion." Wimbush, "We Will Make Our Own," 46. "The Souls of White Folk," conversely, "railed against what he took to be the unique racial perversion foisted on mankind by Western civilization during the nineteenth century." See Lewis, *W. E. B. Du Bois*, 469.

28. Du Bois, *Dark Water*, 17.

> Of them I am singularly clairvoyant. I see in and through them. I view them from unusual points of advantage. Not as a foreigner do I come, for I am native, not foreign, bone of their thought and flesh of their language. Mine is not the knowledge of the traveler or the colonial composite of dear memories, words and wonder.... Rather I see souls undressed and from the back and side. I see the working of their entrails. I know their thoughts and they know that I know. This knowledge makes them embarrassed, now furious.[29]

Du Bois was aware of this so-called whiteness as a sensitive soul.[30] By *sensitive*, I mean to suggest that Du Bois was profoundly aware of social theory and analysis. He used pragmatic philosophy to better understand the reality of truth. For Du Bois, such an enterprise entails tremendous effort and dedication. Still, it is well worth the struggle because one becomes sensitive to the truth about what black people have endured in America. Du Bois embodied this type of thinking and analytical work. By *soul*, I merely wish to highlight that realm of a person for whom light or darkness passes through and exists upon the essence of one's center. It is the core. The very center of human quality. Whatever that quality entails. Within an African-centered worldview, the *soul* is equivalent to divine air.

In *The Souls of Black Folk*, he describes his notion of black double consciousness. As the proposition goes, black people are forced to grapple with a perennial label of *otherness* because they were born within a society that keeps a structural understanding of their *otherness*. Du Bois believed, however, that living in both realms with equal appreciation was possible until his departure to Ghana in 1961. He also understood that such an experience was implausible based on most white people's social structure and sentiment. Therefore, to remedy this moral wrong, Du Bois worked tirelessly to search out, find, study, and agitate elements within a system that reinforced inequality and ignorance among its people. Du Bois complains that societal growth is hindered because of "the deliberately educated ignorance of white schools."[31]

It is highly likely that Du Bois, concluding white schools lacked a balanced appreciation for blackness, also alluded to a more nuanced perspective, which suggests that schools aid in developing human character, ethics,

---

29. Du Bois, *Dark Water*, 17.

30. The first use of the generic noun "white" was in January 1661. See Horne, *Counter-Revolution*, 31.

31. Horne, *Counter-Revolution*, 31.

THE LEGITIMATION OF WHITENESS

and a world perspective. Societal groups are created and kept by these individuals, who also have majority governance, laws, and wealth privileges. Thus, Du Bois ironically attacks a part of himself (i.e., his tethered association with whiteness) because the other part of his makeup prevents the jubilant exuberance and uplift of the equally valued world of his blackness. He used his academic studies in history, science, psychology, anthropology, and religion to construct metaphoric prose to describe American racism's sinister depth and breadth.

Primarily, Du Bois understands white religion (i.e., the religion of whiteness), or white Christianity, to be a "miserable failure."[32] White religion had failed to live out what it professed to be of the highest value. This thought is suitable with a degree of caution. The ideals of Jesus are undoubtedly worthy of contemplation and reflection. Also, one should try to live up to such standards worldwide. By conflating whiteness with a religious experience, Du Bois illuminated America's racist reality for centuries and constructed a religion devoid of spiritual attention to collective human elevation. Instead, the scope was narrowed to race, and emphasizing one race chosen by God would substantiate the claim to divine elevation and expansion. In its most fundamental sense, the religion of whiteness was a faithful practice of ideas that promoted the necessity and privilege of white consumption of the world. He begrudgingly admits, "I am given to understand that whiteness is the ownership of the earth forever and ever, Amen!"[33]

Moreover, there seems to be no end to the white religion's insatiable appetite for more. Increasingly, Du Bois saw this intentional existence toward supremacy grow more vital from one generation to the next. "Wave on Wave," he asserts, "each with increasing virulence, is dashing this new religion of whiteness on the shores of our time."[34] Considering the theory of human culture and its intricate arrival at what is purported to be good and evil, Du Bois said that the *religion of whiteness* had infected every known element of American life. Thus, notions about the goodness of white and the badness of black "are continually rung in picture and story, in newspaper heading and moving-picture, in sermon and school book, until, of course, the King can do no wrong, a White man is always right and a Black

---

32. Du Bois, *Dark Water*, 21.
33. Du Bois, "Souls of White Folk," 924.
34. Du Bois, *Dark Water*, 21.

Man has no rights which a white man is bound to respect."[35] This rather emphatic proposition is a reiteration of what Supreme Court Justice Roger Taney stated in the *Dred Scott* ruling (1857) about black peoples' historical nature in America. The thought, the idea, of black people as inferior had appeared in the Supreme Court's hallowed hall. Du Bois needs to highlight that racial supremacy was not merely a reality destined to be experienced by poor, uneducated whites. Racial supremacy reached the wealthiest and most erudite of white spaces. Social morality was a common way of thinking for most white Americans despite differences in education and wealth.

THE PSYCHOLOGY AND USE OF WHITE PRIVILEGE

Additionally, whiteness is a philosophical *way of being* presumptuous and culturally dismissive. It is a tradition that many whites faithfully practice daily via mental associations. Christopher Collins and Alexander Jun argue that the dominating part of white privilege is indeed mental architecture, which undoubtedly presents with implicit bias, thus making it difficult for white people to visualize their privilege.[36] Whites tend to denounce spaces of privilege and reduce the experience of advantage to determinism. But whiteness, as a social construct, privileges those who exist within its parameters. Because many *good-willed* whites tend to think that the term "racist," when applied to their experience, presents a negative connotation. They defend themselves by asserting that it is unfair to suggest that all whites are racist based on an ideology that was constructed centuries ago. But as Stephanie M. Wildman and Adrienne D. Davis also explain:

> For me to struggle to visualize privilege has most often taken the form of the struggle to see my white privilege. Even as I write about this struggle, I fear that my own racism will make things worse, causing me to do more harm than good. Some readers may be shocked to see a white person contritely acknowledge that she is a racist. I do not say this with pride. I simply believe that no matter how hard I work at not being racist, I still am. Because part of racism is systemic. I benefit from the privilege that I am struggling to see. . . . All whites are racist in this use of the term, because we benefit from systemic white privilege. Generally, whites think of racism as voluntary, intentional conduct, done by horrible others.

---

35. Du Bois, *Dark Water*, 25.
36. Collins and Jun, *White Out*, 4–9.

THE LEGITIMATION OF WHITENESS

> Whites spend a lot of time trying to convince ourselves and each other that we are not racist. A big step would be for whites to admit that we are racist and then to consider what to do about it.[37]

Moreover, Robin DiAngelo's *White Fragility* acknowledges the difficulty associated with white people embracing implicit bias. For DiAngelo, privileged whites work from within what sociologist Joe Feagin described as a *white racial frame*.[38] This lens purports white supremacy in mass media, politics, education, and religion. Additionally, this perennial frame of reference for white constructs, regulates, and sustains cultural signifiers that perpetuate notions of race superiority and inferiority. This degree of "whiteness," as Du Bois would conclude, "is the ownership of the earth forever and ever, Amen!"[39] Whiteness is so pervasive that even *well-intentioned whites* are subject to black space exploitation. In 1959, for instance, John Howard Griffin wondered, "What is it like to experience discrimination based on skin color?"[40] He later digested medication that would change his pigmentation from white to black skin. Although Griffin is lauded as being one who used his whiteness to better understand blackness, he nevertheless could cease taking the pills and revert to a privileged state of being, a state that blacks do not have the luxury of experiencing.

The mental construction that white privilege scholars present as a fundamental basis of invisibility is what Du Bois in 1935 termed the *psychological wage*.[41] He argues that although white laborers received low wages during Reconstruction, their plights were not coupled with the prospect of being lynched, raped, mutilated, or even socially ostracized. Being born into a system that was constructed to bequeath a certain degree of privilege for poor whites was enough to embrace the low wage and still put oneself above that of the wealthiest blacks. The oft-stated mantra that *green is the only color that matters* is no doubt a fallacy when experiencing life with black skin. For instance, early eighteenth-century black millionaire John Drew had to use white proxies "to perform financial transactions to avoid being excluded based on race."[42]

---

37. Wildman and Davis, "Making Systems of Privilege Visible," 142.
38. DiAngelo, *White Fragility*, 35.
39. Du Bois, "Souls of White Folk," 924.
40. Griffin, *Black Like Me*, 1.
41. Du Bois, *Black Reconstruction*, 700.
42. Wills, *Black Fortunes*, x–xv.

Suppose one feels as though an eighteenth-century example is too ancient. In that case, Lawrence Otis Graham's experience acknowledges that his notion of black elitism and wealth was challenged when he had to write a *Nine Rules of Survival* treatise when his son was accosted at an elite academy. His son reported that two men pulled up in a car as he was walking and glaringly asked, "Are you the only nigger at Mellon Academy?"[43] After hearing the fear in his son's voice, Graham was convinced that economic privilege and Ivy League affiliation were still not enough to secure an unbiased status in white space. One rule warns his children to avoid enjoying a pleasant stroll in any residential neighborhood after sundown. And never carry a metallic object that could be mistaken as a weapon.[44] But such a way of existing must be psychologically exhausting. There is not much freedom shown in such an experience; nevertheless, there seems to be psychological freedom associated with blacks who are granted permission to live in white space, although socially constrained, yet they relish being tethered to a system in which they can *move on up*. This reality of black access was portrayed in the 1970s sitcom *The Jeffersons* (e.g., such blacks moved on up and finally got a piece of the proverbial American pie).[45]

In "Privilege as Paradox," Allan Johnson asserts, "The concept of oppression points to social forces that tend to 'press' upon people and hold them down, to hem them in and block their pursuit of a good life. Just as privilege tends to open doors of opportunity, oppression tends to slam them shut." The former thought is true regarding privilege, which is having the ability to open doors. Still, privilege can also close doors, which inherently situates privilege categorically within the same typology as that of oppression. Johnson furthers his argument by suggesting that to be oppressed, one must belong to an oppressed category; for instance, "Men cannot be oppressed as men, just as whites cannot be oppressed as whites or heterosexuals as heterosexuals because a group can be oppressed only if there exists another group that has the power to oppress them."[46] This sort of thinking and behavior is problematic as it negates the significance of individualized power and relegates the group dynamic as the dominant comparison metric, from which the individual appears as a representation. Yet, it is reasonable to argue that whites cannot be oppressed as whites,

---

43. Graham, "I Taught My Black Kids," 182.
44. Graham, "I Taught My Black Kids," 182.
45. Nicholl et al., *Jeffersons*.
46. Johnson, "Privilege as Paradox," 148.

due in large part to the dominance that whites have over society. This does not mean, however, that white individuals are exempt from the notion of oppressive suffering. White abolitionists *suffered* because of aligning with slaves in their quest for freedom. In this same context, white people used their privilege for good, and many slaves were helped by privileged whites during slavery.

White privilege, however, overshadows the insidious ploys of black privilege as the amount of space used to oppress blacks is greater than the sum of stratified space within black reality. Although white privilege, in and of itself, is designed to be used for destructive purposes, the energy of such privilege can be transmuted and used for the uplift of the black race. When white privilege is used for good, it has the potential to create spaces in which underprivileged and oppressed blacks garner opportunities to thrive and live out their humanity in the fullness of joy and abundance.

8

A CULTURAL PARADOX
The "Traditional" Black Church
(Spirits of Rebellion and Abandonment)

AT ITS CORE, THE black church began before plantation living and the modern civil rights era.[1] The black church, with the undergirding principles of defiance and violent resistance, started the moment two differentiated Africans were chained together and the decision was made, despite the potential animosity the two Africans may have shared against each other based on tribal affiliation, that they must work together to survive and obtain freedom. This early rendition of togetherness was established with the first African sorrow songs, steadfast moans and groans, protests, and rebellions; togetherness was experienced in high volume during the slave ship experience as well as on land when African tribalism was adapted to a

---

1. Gayraud S. Wilmore's categorization of the black church entails three movements. First, the newly enslaved Africans sought religion together to survive in the seventeenth and eighteenth centuries, especially seen in the development of black-influenced churches in the 1700s in Savannah, Georgia; South Carolina; and Tidewater, Virginia. Second, the black middle-class church assimilated more into American society between the mid-1850s and the first quarter of the twentieth century. Third, which overlaps with the former, is a period that Professor Wilmore refers to as a *paradigm of liberation*, which consists of a direct leadership role from black religious structures in efforts to carve more political, economic, and social power for blacks. I am a student of such framing. My contribution as a scholar is to suggest adding two centuries to the initial move, which places the inception of the black church in the mid-1400s. See Wilmore, *Pragmatic Spirituality*, 50.

codified cultural, black-bonded humanity, which would produce stories of resistance for future generations of enslaved blacks to reference. However, the spirit of resistance would eventually be replaced with a spirit of abandonment as one generation after the other moved closer to a compromised way of surviving in the *New World*.

RESISTANCE

Resistance for the enslaved entailed a struggle to remain human, to remain alive (to survive).[2] The initial revolts in the *New World* were likely led primarily by religious leaders, royalty, and tribal warriors.[3] In addition, secret societies such as the Poro and Sande were significant social organizations that produced leaders who would someday lead slave ship revolts. Taking on such leadership roles makes sense, as the Poro and Sande secret societies were mandatory social obligations for Africans.[4] In essence, such leaders had been groomed since childhood to occupy such a position of authority.

Led by these highly intuitive Africans, the enslaved Africans onboard the slave ships followed orders with precision; when they would select the perfect time to attack, it would be brutal and a very intimate experience.[5] For a rebellion to have a semblance of chance, slaves, according to Winston McGowan, needed a safe environment to plan, an element of surprise, numerical advantage, and deficiencies in the ship's crew.[6] Onboard the *Amistad* on July 2, 1839, prompted by the prospects of being eaten by the white slavers, the slaves rose, with the aid of little girls handing out machetes and of Lubos of the Poro Society. Cinque reminded his fellow captives that they were not slaves but warriors. Feeling the rhythm of African solidarity,

---

2. Woodson, *Negro in Our History,* 89.

3. McGowan, "Origins," 88.

4. Tobin and Raymond, *Hidden in Plain View,* 38.

5. 1509: *Nau Fieis de Deus* (Portugal). Unsuccessful. 1532: *Misericordia* (Portugal). Capt. Estevao Carreiro. Between São Tomé Island and Elmina. All but three crew members killed. Successful—freedom? 1571: (Spain). West Indies. The Slaves "slit the throats of the crew." Successful—freedom? May 1713: *Victorious Anne* (England). Cape Coast (Gold Coast). All but seven crew members killed. The ship was blown up in the insurrection. Successful—freedom? Feb. 1772: *Ferrers/Farres* (London, England). Capt. Francis Messervy/Messerve. Middle Passage, eighty slaves and one crew member killed. Unsuccessful. Slaves tried to revolt twice, once landed in Jamaica. See E. Taylor, *If We Must Die,* 124.

6. E. Taylor, *If We Must Die,* 82.

Cinque asked, "Who is for war?"[7] After a successful rebellion, as is customary in Mende warfare, "The warriors danced, yelled, and beheaded the captain in their customary rituals of war called *kootoo*."[8]

The enslaved warriors onboard the *Amistad* carried on a tradition that dates back three hundred years. In 1526, for instance, the first group of enslaved Africans on North American soil fought the Spanish enslavers at some location near present-day South Carolina,[9] and the Wolof slaves were the first to physically resist on a significant scale in Hispaniola in 1521.[10] Slaves, in 1526, rebelled against Lucas Vasquez de Ayllon and fled the settlement he started.[11] As a means of deterring similar behavior, Mexico City's first viceroy, Antonio de Mendonza, executed the leaders of the first slave conspiracy in 1537.[12] In 1683, enslaved Africans on St. Helena rose together and killed the governor.[13] Seven whites were killed in Newton, Long Island, by a small group of slaves in 1708. The "men were hanged, and the woman burned."[14] In 1730, three hundred enslaved Africans in Virginia ran away from their enslavers and joined together in the Great Dismal Swamp.[15] In South Carolina in 1791, slaves were sentenced to death by the method of being burned alive at the exact location where it is alleged they murdered a white overseer.[16] Another slave in South Carolina killed an overseer with an ax and was hanged as due punishment on the same day.[17]

There are also occasions in which one discovers enslaved Africans working against other enslaved Africans on slave ships during rebellions. On the *Eagle* (1704), during the revolt, slaves nearly tossed the captain and crew overboard. Rebels hit the captain with a piece of wood and were going to hit him again but were hindered when a fellow slave intervened and blocked the blow with his arm, breaking it. The ship's doctor treated the slave, who was granted freedom upon his arrival in Virginia. In 1841, nineteen male slaves aboard *The Creole* rushed the crew and fought ferociously

---

7. Rediker, *Amistad*, 73.
8. Rediker, *Amistad*, 78.
9. Wood, *Black Majority*, 3.
10. Landers, "Cimarrón and Citizen," 117.
11. Wood, *Black Majority*, 3.
12. Landers, "Cimarrón and Citizen," 118.
13. Horne, *Counter-Revolution*, 26.
14. Aptheker, *American Negro*, 169.
15. Richter, *Before the Revolution*, 353.
16. Wood, *Black Majority*, 278.
17. Wood, *Black Majority*, 286.

in the dark for hours. All one could hear were the screams of both whites and blacks.[18] Slave revolts onboard the slave ship were not spontaneous, and revolts developed into controlled anger and hatred toward people who looked like their captives. This association was no doubt passed down generationally.

Many militarily trained Africans appeared to be focused rebels. They would have been accustomed to planning out a surprise attack, but what made many revolts successful was how enslaved Africans worked together. For instance, an enslaved woman on the English slave ship *Robert* in 1721, off the shore of Sierra Leone, detected that the crew was small enough that enslaved Africans could, if given the right tools, exert a successful rebellion. She collected weapons and passed them along, and the uprising began. The fighting Africans managed to circumvent several guards, but unfortunately, it was insufficient. The rebellion was finally quashed, and the "woman was hanged by her thumbs and whipped and sliced with knives until dead."[19] Even African cooks aboard the slave ship tried to give aid by supplying specific tools to fellow blacks, freeing themselves from their chains.[20]

Every village had its musical experts, so musicians, singers, and the like found themselves onboard the dreaded slave ship.[21] Rich in traditional African ways of being, music was also used as a conduit for rebellion. Drumming, for instance, a key element in African musicology, allowed Africans to communicate and send complex messages over distances.[22] In fact, it is said that off the coast of southern Ghana, one can listen to the rhythm of the African drum from miles away at night.[23] An instrument played with palms, fingers, and sticks, the membranophone, or drum, was carved from a tree trunk and came in many sizes.[24] African drums are used to call the spirits of the ancestors through specific rhythms and vibration frequencies.[25] Angolans even used drums to make oral arguments before

---

18. Slaves began to revolt the moment they were aboard the ship. See Hendrick and Hendrick, *Creole Mutiny*, 4, 84.

19. Hendrick and Hendrick, *Creole Mutiny*, 90.

20. Hendrick and Hendrick, *Creole Mutiny*, 79. The occupation of black cook began in the 1700s. Rediker, *Slaveship*, 60.

21. Southern, *Music*, 8.

22. Craton, *Testing the Chains*, 47.

23. A. Bailey, *African Voices*, 1.

24. Southern, *Music*, 9–10.

25. Mustakeem, *Slavery at Sea*, 119.

the chief regarding legal matters.[26] The Stono Rebels, led by Angolans, used the drum to call on the ancestral spirits to assist the slaves in meeting at a specific locale to organize and engage the battle ahead of them.[27] To be sure, the war drum spoke utter deference to deities and summoned warriors to the call for battle.[28]

Resistance also came in the form of sabotage in which the slave deliberately broke tools, refused to work, and took part in verbal insubordination, which was a way in which the enslaved sought to break the system that undergirded their social despair.[29] Some slaves were branded several separate times as they moved toward the coast to the ultimate destination, the slave ship. It took several sailors to hold the ferocious African captives. Once subdued by the fire, a hot iron symbol of ownership was seared into the skin of the African slave. The brand, as it is called, touched small children as well. It was likely that the children, however, would receive their brand on the buttocks while adults were tagged on the shoulder, breast, thigh, and stomach.[30] Africans resisted this treatment from the outset.

Africans also resisted the European threat on land by utilizing their knowledge and wisdom of the African terrain. As slave raiders chased Africans and forced whole communities to uproot and create something different, fleeing Africans used spikes that were covered and undetectable to hinder the onslaught of European aggression. Additionally, hunted Africans created red herrings that would seem to lead slavers to the precise locale of unaware slaves, only for the slavers to find that they had gone down a path carved by Africans as a deterrent from their central location. As an additional measure, Africans set up patrol systems to guard their perimeter.[31] The Masina, for instance, created alarm systems.[32] As was the case for the Gurunsi villages, entrances to villages were built extremely low.[33] The Aja people sought refuge from the aggressive slave trade in Quidah, Allada,

26. Southern, *Music*, 7.
27. Horne, *Counter-Revolution*, 110–11.
28. Reis, *Slave Rebellion in Brazil*, 41.
29. Reis, *Slave Rebellion in Brazil*, 287.
30. E. Taylor, *If We Must Die*, 23.
31. E. Taylor, *If We Must Die*, 123.
32. Klein, "Defensive Strategies," 73.
33. Some as low as seventy centimeters. See Klein, "Defensive Strategies," 73.

and Abomey by relocating to the Lacustrine. Many were captured, however, by raiders from Dahomey.[34]

Africans used the land to defend themselves from further European encroachment. At times, this defense came in the form of poisoning. Jamaica was a prominent hub for poisoning. Poison was one way they tried to balance their fight against slavery. Moreover, it has been suggested that every white person in Virginia in the 1760s knew a free person who had been killed by a slave. Whites were so worried about being poisoned by slaves that they had nightmares.[35] Gerald Horne notes, "Troubling for the colonists was the idea that poisoning slaveholders had spread to Massachusetts by 1755, as two Africans—male and female—were executed in Charlestown for doing so."[36] They planted venomous plants along routes whites took.[37] Poison was considered a felony by the Negro Act of 1740. By 1751, more clauses had been added. For instance, it was a felony for slaves to teach other slaves about herbs and plant use.

Suicide was an act of rebellion but was the last resort. Jumping overboard on the slave ship, for instance, was a finale that many Africans dreamed of. If desperate slaves were halted from jumping overboard, some made the conscious choice to starve themselves to death. This did not go over well with the slavers, so those who tried to starve themselves were "force-fed through funnel, whipped, lips scorched by coals, teeth broken, mouth forced open with the aid of device known as the Speculum Oris." As a final act of desperation, slaves "refused medicine, hanged themselves with bits of clothing, suffocated, and smashed their head against walls of ship holds."[38] Orlando Patterson, while discussing the slave culture of Jamaica, also reasons that suicide was prevalent because slaves believed that if they cut their throats, they would return home to Africa.[39] But while enslaved, a community (i.e., church) would be developed to not only press toward freedom but to also tend to the human needs of the enslaved while moving along the tedious journey.

---

34. Soumonni, "Lacustrine," 7.

35. Horne, *Counter-Revolution*, 237.

36. Horne, *Counter-Revolution*, 157.

37. Dedde shrub (*acacia ataxantha*) were also planted. See Gueye, "Impact of the Slave Trade," 56.

38. E. Taylor, *If We Must Die*, 37, 38.

39. Patterson, *Sociology of Slavery*, 195.

THE AUTHENTIC BLACK COMMUNITY AND RELIGIOUS INFLUENCES

In Cuba, Francisco Gonzalez, an enslaved African, saw another enslaved African on the plantation and referred to him as *camarada* (i.e., comrade).[40] *Cabildos,* a town or community council where issues are discussed and debated, was a unifying element for various Africans enslaved in Cuba. Matt Childs contends that these *cabildos* helped the members with a carved space where they could be authentic about their treatment as slaves.[41] Slave runaway communities, known as maroons or *Quilombos,* were spaces where, according to João José Reis, the African *collective spirit* was renewed and emboldened to rebel against their oppressors. They also frequented these mobile spaces as a means to cure maladies.[42] And they fought together. Several hundred, dressed in what the local police called white war garments, marched the streets of Salvador as a display of togetherness and unification.[43] Bahia was undoubtedly known for its unified rebellious slaves.[44] For instance, the black practice of fist-to-fist connection and salutation was likely first seen with Bahian slaves. When they greeted one another, "they struck their rings as a sign of brotherhood."[45]

Passed down by early African enslaved religious leaders, rebellion stories provided a means by which some enslaved communities developed the ability to survive the trauma associated with enslavement while also creating a sense of purpose as being a new codified black being.[46] As time in the

---

40. Childs, *1812 Aponte Rebellion,* 56–57.

41. Childs, *1812 Aponte Rebellion,* 188.

42. Reis, *Slave Rebellion in Brazil,* 41–42.

43. The white garments "were [a] long frock called an *abada* in Bahia, an *aqbada* or *agbada* in Yorubaland." Reis, *Slave Rebellion in Brazil,* 103.

44. Graden, "This City," 136.

45. Reis, *Slave Rebellion in Brazil,* 104. Kende rings were worn on the thumb and the third or fourth finger of the left hand.

46. Coalesced blacks, those who chose to rebuff notions of white world acquiescence, fought with everything at their disposal to remain true to their identity as cosmic beings with divine privileges to be free because, as they understood the cosmos, God had given them those privileges, even if violence became the ultimate resolution. Uncoalesced hybrid blacks, those who had become ashamed of their black-skin affiliation on both a conscious and unconscious level, attempted to compromise their cultural inheritance to gain more wealth, freedom, and prestige within the white world. They used people who looked like them to elevate as far as possible above the association of their black skin, a *New World* social implication. The first process of capture, resistance, and semi-capitulation proved to be a pivotal experience; it was in the belly of the slave ship, however, that

A CULTURAL PARADOX

New World passed, diversified enslaved African peoples gradually moved away from African traditions that once divided them; instead, they placed more energy on ideals that strengthened this new bond, such as structured cosmologies, meditation, and ancestral worship.[47] With forward thinking, the new black community created adapted ways of existing and expressing their religious and spiritual inheritances. Such an experience, for instance, is seen in the development of the spiritual system of Vodun.

There is no specific date or time, but at some point in historical memory, it can be estimated that legitimate priests, prophets, and diviners, men and women who received formal and traditional education for several years and who were privileged with the birth rite, became significantly diminished as the African slave trade flourished, especially during the Golden Era, 1700–1803.[48] Regardless of their specialty, the religious figures shared a common theme of being the interpreter between the visible and invisible worlds.[49] In times of trouble and existential concern, the people consorted with religious leaders to seek a remedy by eliminating or explaining an issue.

The process of enslavement certainly qualified as an existential concern for Africans. Undoubtedly, throughout the several phases of the

---

dreadful dungeon of doom, where once differentiated free Africans came to terms with that moment with what Harding also refers to as a *matrix of continental oneness*. Harding, *There is a River*, 4. The enslaved Africans forged a new identity in a shared cultural bondedness of struggle with other enslaved Africans. They forged a lived experience of perennial resistance against a global enterprise of European domination.

47. Chireau, *Black Magic*, 37, 41.

48. Scholars within the field of black religious studies agree that African spiritual traditions, although not entirely in ritualistic form, survived in the minds of the first generation of Africans who were enslaved and transported to the *New World*. Every element of African society experienced the reality of chattel enslavement. Kings, queens, traditional healers, witches, sorcerers, warriors, and religious figures eventually found themselves shackled together on board a slave ship en route to the *New World*.

49. In traditional African religious practices, a duality of power is constantly at odds with each other. The *wontfe*, the good conventional healer, has an extensive knowledge of herbal practices, outlining both the good and bad uses. The *wontfulo*, the bad traditional healer, was open to being paid to kill and harm people. This duality of power struggle would also be seen in the *New World* as a negotiated force to combat African status as slaves, particularly between the Obeah and practitioners of Myalism. Myalism, it could be argued, because it come after the introduction of Obeah, is a direct counter to the antics and practices of the Obeah. Indeed, it was. Myalism is anti-witchcraft, so when an African wishes to catch someone's spirit, Myalism soon becomes a method by which the doctor could also release a captured spirit. See Patterson, *Sociology of Slavery*, 184; Ray, *African Religions*, 72.

Middle Passage, from the first capture to the belly of the slave ship, Africans would have been seeking guidance from these figures. This is especially true of enslaved priests, as their position of authority was viewed as second only to the chief. When the dominant office of the priest became a lingering memory, and the people were left without their traditional ways of addressing their concern of enslavement, Africans familiar with some religious notions and practices that were perhaps gleaned from legitimate priestly functionaries used a mixture of religious belief and tools to create what became known as the new black religious leader, Obeah in the West Indies, for instance, under the spiritual system and direction of Vodun.

Slavers tried to repress the religion, or way of being, of Vodun because it was associated with rebellion and resistance.[50] It took shape during the 1700s with the mixed religious traditions of the West Coast Africans (e.g., the Fon) and the West Indies transplants.[51] As Robert Farris Thompson notes, "Vodun was Africa re-blended. The encounter of the classical religions of Kongo, Dahomey, and Yorubaland gave rise to a creole religion."[52] However, only the most prominent traditions from western Nigeria and eastern Benin Republic survived the trek across the Atlantic. For instance, deities such as the Supreme Olorun, Oshan (goddess of love), Oshoosi (god of hunting), Eshu (spirit of individuality and change), Ifa (god of divination), Ogun (god of iron), and Yemoja (goddess of the seas), with Eshu-Elegbara being the primary in the black Atlantic world.[53]

Obeah, becoming the mixture of priestly knowledge and willingness to use said knowledge to inflict harm on a person, became highly respected in the *New World* by both slavers and enslaved Africans. Respect in this regard need not equate to a sense of acceptance; instead, for instance, slavers respected the influence of African religion and religious leaders enough to understand the need for its abrupt denunciation and eradication. But something survived underneath the social pressure of exposure and punishment. The slaves learned to move and exist as a collective mind despite

---

50. The first fifteen thousand Africans arrived in Haiti in 1517. Vodun practices would also find their way onto the island. It was a practice forbidden by law. The Vodun priest, Boukman Dutty, and the priestess, Cecile Fatiman, Mambo, were linked together in 1791 to ignite a rebellion that was considered the first and only large-scale black rebellion that was successful. The instruction and practices of Vodun undergirded this effort.

51. Genovese, *Roll, Jordan, Roll*, 220.

52. Thompson, *Flash*, 164.

53. Thompson, *Flash*, xvi–xix.

the all-consuming arm of their enslavers. And the Obeah, men and women, led in this regard.

The Obeah also exercised power by "preventing, detecting, and punishing crimes among the slaves."[54] In Jamaica, for instance, Obeah was a practice of sorcery that focused on the needs of a client who had a request to manipulate and even kill people by way of herbal concoctions. Such Obeah was likely from Dahomey and was of a direct origin.[55] Obeah was distinguishable as practitioners carried wooden emblems of authority with "carved serpent twisted round them and Negroes were fearful of these sticks."[56] They had every right to be, and with these emblems of authority came a practice known as shadow catching. Orlando Patterson reasons that the Jamaican practice of shadow catching is amazingly similar to that of the Ga people.

> Among the Ga people, the essential aspect of the human personality was the *Susuma*. The exact word Susuma was also used for shadow among these people. Closely related to the susuma or shadow is the *Kla* concept, which designates the life-blood of a person; when the Kla leaves the individual, he dies. We are told further that a bad medicine-man, for a fee, will call upon a victim's Kla or Susumu and either tie it up with a string or gaze at it in a bowl of water and, on seeing it, stab it through the heart.[57]

The Obeah used a variety of elements to aid them in casting spells, interpreting the unseen, and crime detection. For instance, the snake and its teeth were of value. This makes sense as it has been seen that the Obeah marked the snake as of religious significance by aligning and associating it with their emblem of power.[58] By way of authority, Obeah investigated crimes among the slaves. Upon being briefed on a crime, the Obeah would assemble all slaves to the grave of the vanquished, for instance, and for the guilty party, after consuming some dirt, the "stomach should swell and burst."[59] Whenever and wherever the slaves rebelled on the island, Obeah

---

54. Patterson, *Sociology of Slavery*, 190.
55. Patterson, *Sociology of Slavery*, 188.
56. Patterson, *Sociology of Slavery*, 190.
57. Patterson, *Sociology of Slavery*, 189.
58. Obeah also resorted to the use of "Blood, feathers, Parrots Beaks, Dog's Teeth, Alligator's Teeth, Broken bottles, Grave dirt, Rum, Egg Shell." Patterson, *Sociology of Slavery*, 191.
59. Patterson, *Sociology of Slavery*, 191.

was a primary leader. They blessed their endeavor, cursed their enemies, addressed issues of betrayal, and handed out fetishes and emblems of their individualized power.[60]

By the 1750s, the African religious/spiritual leader, with emphasis on resistance and rebellion, gave way to a new generation of *slave preachers*. The African position of authority was comprised of spiritual leaders' intent on freeing enslaved people from the experience of white domination. Such people wanted nothing to do with any accoutrements associated with a *New World* mentality. However, the Christianization of the Africans assisted in transitioning the rebellious African leader into a more controlled and innocuous slave preacher. All slave preachers, to be sure, did not fully embrace all of the proposed religious doctrines that their owners placed before them. Nat Turner is an excellent example of this new blended enslaved religious figure. He used African religious and spiritual traditions (e.g., reading and interpreting the stars and sky for divine messages) and the Bible to further the pattern of his early forebears. A tradition of resistance and rebellion.

After Nat Turner's rebellion in 1831, slave preaching declined significantly as it became illegal. By the end of the 1890s, a new black religious faction had taken over black people's communal and social organization. What has become known as the traditional black church was born out of this movement. The conventional moniker is perhaps associated with the public renunciation by some black preachers of ties to the old and unlearned way of existing as black people in the *New World*. For the African religious leader and uncompromising slave preacher, tradition meant embracing the notion of community for all blacks. For the compromising slave preacher and emerging twentieth-century black preacher, the community meant a selective class of blacks.

ABANDONMENT

As a result of chattel enslavement, "blackness took on a new meaning" for the African enslaved.[61] The meaning, of course, entailed being thrust into a cultural experience of black togetherness. Africans marched toward the sea together, stayed in the barracoons together, and eventually were loaded as cargo aboard the slave ship together and died fighting together.

60. Patterson, *Sociology of Slavery*, 192.
61. Berlin, *Making of African America*, 55.

A CULTURAL PARADOX

Unfortunately, in the early 1900s, we saw a hard pivot within black communal/religious spaces. Denominational groups began to distance the black experience from functions of slave religion, a period Gayraud S. Wilmore described as the deradicalization of the black church, especially with the death of the iconic bishop, Henry M. Turner, in 1915.[62] This social vehicle of abandonment created space for the early twentieth-century black church to emerge ideally as a vehicle to address the social needs of survival and attempted assimilation into the white world of convenience and opportunity. Thus, the focus went from noncompliance and rebellion to acquaintance social indifference and abandonment. The new black leaders were busy carving individualized space within a sub-world that provided quasi-power to otherwise powerless people. As Henry Mitchell notes:

> Churches in the North, especially were prone to avoid electing deacons who were not yet free. And there was constant awareness of class distinctions even though the churches of the North tended to be strongly anti-slavery, and active in the Underground Railroad. Yet black-on-black paternalism by the freed was not uncommon in many circles, even among some active abolitionists. In a history of African American Episcopalians written by Father George F. Brag in 1922, class distinctions were clearly affirmed among African Americans, all the way back to the very beginning of organized congregations.[63]

As time progressed and religious black space became more foundational, blacks unconsciously began to display a morbid stratification in their sub-world. Elliott M. Rudwick notes, "At the end of the nineteenth century, W. E. B. Du Bois accused black religious spaces of being 'useless' and lacking a degree of concern for the education of African Americans."[64] Some black religious leaders posited that slave religion, although beneficial in its beginning phase, included uncouth blacks who lacked a certain cultural sophistication. As E. Franklin Frazier would later posit:

> The attitude of educated leaders of even Methodist and Baptist churches was expressed by a Bishop in the African Methodist Episcopal Church even before Emancipation. He opposed the singing of the Spirituals, which he described as "corn field ditties" and songs of "fist and heel worshippers" and said that the ministry

---

62. Wilmore, *Black Religion*, 187–227.
63. Mitchell, *Black Church Beginnings*, 72.
64. Rudwick, *W. E. B. Du Bois*, 26.

of the A.M.E. Church must drive out such "heathenish mode of worship" or "drive out all intelligence and refinement."[65]

MORBID CONSCIOUSNESS AND THE DEATH OF THE SLAVE PREACHING TRADITION

This mode of thinking permeated well into the mid-twentieth century when Dr. King presented this matter as a deterrent to black racial uplift. He says emphatically:

> Two types of Negro churches have failed to provide bread. One burns with emotionalism, and the other freezes with classism.... Worship at its best is a social experience in which people of all levels of life come together to affirm their oneness and unity under God. At midnight men are altogether ignored because of their limited education, or they are given bread that has been hardened by the winter of morbid class consciousness.[66]

Dr. King shows two privileged groups within the same black subworld; both groups understand their position to be relevant spaces of privilege, but King warns that both positions are antithetical to the true togetherness that existed in the initial stages of slave unification. The educated black, according to King, was insensitive to the degree to which unlettered slaves contributed to the establishment of the black church; on the other hand, King admonishes the unlettered for being insensitive to the contributions that educated blacks provided in the organizational stage of the black church. It is interesting to note, when speaking out on issues such as American militarism and capitalism, it was often posited, from both black and white writers and political pundits, that Dr. King was working outside the scope of his ability. It was argued that he "is getting out of his depth." But King was merely following the dialectical dance of his forebears, using both his head and heart to address social ills of his era. A sentiment that was associated with the early black church.[67]

Because of social isolation, the early black church provided an outlet for universal frustration and formed a basis for social cohesion. "The organization of the Black Church," C. D. Coleman notes, "was the first

65. Frazier, *Negro Church*, 37.
66. M. King, "Knock at Midnight," 501–2.
67. Baldwin, *Arc of Truth*, 163.

A CULTURAL PARADOX

important step forward in preserving their ethnic culture and developing black consciousness."[68] To this point, C. Eric Lincoln contends that the black church is universal.[69] It stands for all blacks. Peter Paris, however, argued that blacks often focused on individual pursuits rather than racial uplift; paradoxically, this is why the church was set up and organized.[70] In 2010, Eddie Glaude forthrightly argued that the black church is dead because it no longer functions following its ontological trajectory of rebellion and resistance.[71] For Glaude, the contemporary black church does not reflect the prophetic energy of its past, nor can it. Moreover, for Glaude, the role of the black church has been, since its ontological founding, to address the social issues that affect blacks on the *national stage*.

Due to the experience of morbid consciousness, representatives of the institution have not always promoted its philosophical essence. However, this long-standing struggle has created tension for the black church as a social change institution. For instance, in 1898, Rev. Henry Hugh Proctor challenged the black churches in Atlanta, Georgia, to set aside the yearnings for the frenzy of black sacred worship to focus on issues such as providing aid to the New Florence Critten Home for girls.[72]

For Dr. King, the black church had become as harmful as the forces of evil that it purported to combat. Marvin A. McMickle echoes this sentiment when he states, "Equal attention must be given to the obvious, but often overlooked, evils and injustices that occur within the [black] preacher's own racial and/or ethnic community."[73] Although Dr. King fundamentally believed that blacks were essentially divided into groups, he nevertheless professed that they ought to work together for the common good of the race. This was the purest example of God's beloved community for King. To visualize the morbidity of black consciousness fully, it is beneficial to understand how group division originated within the black church community.

As a cultural metaphor of identity, the early black church bears out a type of psychic togetherness that manifests once an enslaved African from one tribe is tied, chained, and connected to another enslaved African from a different tribe and speaks a foreign language.

68. Coleman, "Agenda for the Black Church," 188.
69. Lincoln, *Black Church Since Frazier*, 116.
70. Paris, *Social Teaching*, 57.
71. Glaude, "Black Church Is Dead."
72. Du Bois, *Some Efforts of American Negroes*, 51.
73. McMickle, *Where Have All the Prophets*, 18.

THE PROBLEM OF BLACK SKIN

Situational oppression forced the enslaved to work together, embrace a new form of unity, and try to contextualize their experience through universal African ways of meaning, knowing, and existing in the *New World*.[74] This effort was initially led by legitimate priests, sorcerers, royalty, and warriors. When the legitimate priests and dubious sorcerers consolidated their powers to effectively combat the psychic forces of white domination, a new era was born, and the saga of religious leaders would eventually become a staple in the black social analysis of survival.

By the 1730s, the traditional black preacher, who was a manipulator, intellectual, troublemaker, and privileged individual[75] in America, carried on the heritage of dealing with the concerns of the community, but the integration of white Christian instruction began to dilute the message of what it means to be free; as a result, a lot of slave preaching focused on freedom in the here-after. By the late 1800s and early 1900s, there was a desire for some black preachers to disassociate with anything that had to do with African spirituality and belief systems.

Thus, the era in which the slave preaching tradition was based on the liberation and freedom of oppressed blacks was essentially replaced with a tradition of assimilation. I assert that Dr. King was the last preacher, with public and international influence, to lead black people within the scope of the slave preaching tradition of his earlier forbears. Dr. King was assassinated in 1968. Now, considering the degree of oppression inflicted upon blacks since the death of King, one must wonder. Where is the *culturally engaged and protesting* contemporary black church?

---

74. The goal of placing sand in the newly enslaved mouths was not done merely to appease the psychological urges of those eating the sand; the sand, as a representation of Africa herself, became both a physical and spiritual symbol of progeny. If the African was forced into enslavement, the essence of Africa herself was also to become involved and bear, nurture, protect, provide, and guide her children trapped in a world of abrupt chaos. Becoming one with the ground of everything that Africa means to the Africans should be considered as one thinks about and through the problem of the twenty-first-century black struggle for freedom. And by an epigenetic transmission of cultural oneness, what it means to the descendants of those who ate the proverbial sand of Africa. It should be noted from the outset that Africans, filled with memories of ancient wisdom regarding warfare, statecraft, philosophy, literature, social order, astronomy, cosmology, language, ethics, values, and spiritual beliefs (e.g., the land), became captives in the foreign experience and enterprise of chattel enslavement, yet were astute enough to create a cultural metaphor, an ancestral guidepost as it were, for black people to follow. In a sense, the message was to eat the land, digest the land, and remember from which Africans have come.

75. Stallworth, *Existential*, 56.

9

THE ESSENCE OF THE MATTER
(The *Thing*)

THE CENTRAL ISSUE FACING black people today is not racism in and of itself; instead, the problem of black skin is associated with three phenomena. The first deals with the difficulty level of transcending into a deeper analysis of race construction. This process is facilitated by engaging in several fields of study and dissecting the lived experience of black skin based on objective notions regarding the interrelatedness of religion, moral belief, society, and the individual network of influence. The second deals with spirituality, consciousness, and energy manipulation (i.e., technology). The third deals with the United States government and its affiliated military-industrial complex (MIC). First, let us review the conceptual depth of the *Thing*.

DIG, YOUNG MAN, DIG!
(THE DEPTH OF THE THING)

In March 1928, Roland A. Barton, a young aspiring social activist and a very mature high school sophomore from South Bend, Indiana, wrote to the towering figure and brilliant intellectual W. E. B. Du Bois, in earnest, with a confident and humble inquiry requesting an explanation as to why *The Crisis*, the "Official Organ of the National Association for the Advancement of Colored People," would use the word "Negro," a word young Roland argues should be abolished altogether, rather than use the name

"American," to designate a more socially integrated black. It seemed proper for young Roland to rid himself of the language used as a dehumanizing device to undermine black folk's significance and worth.[1] To this end, Roland should be commended on two fronts, if not many more. First, he is a young black male situated in an era where many of his peers would not have *been* afforded the privilege of being a high school sophomore, let alone articulate and debate issues of significant worth for black people. Second, he is aware that the black social world is influenced heavily by white social constructions, but he also hints at the nonwhite collaboration in the same experience. Barton also finds it disturbing that a journal that purports to be a tool for social and cultural enlightenment, with the leading black intellectual on matters of race progression as its editor-in-chief,[2] would continue to use language anathema to the mission of the journal and the editor's claim of progressive race thinking.

Suppose Roland Barton's letter to Du Bois is considered an artifact of valid cultural criticism. In that case, a severe interrogation of race construction and constitution as it were,[3] Du Bois's response to the letter, in his traditional adroitness, must then be viewed in the vein of a concerned parent who corrects and disciplines a child but also fills the gap of knowledge that presented the cause for the correction. Nevertheless, this is done to set up the proper perspective for pursuing the essence of a matter. Therefore, in a poignant and concerned tone, he cautions the young black social thinker, "Do not at the outset of your career make the all-too-common error of mistaking names for things."[4] "Names," argues Du Bois, "are only conventional signs for identifying things. Things are the reality that counts."[5] Indeed, the *Thing*, the essence of a matter, is of most concern.

---

1. Du Bois, "Name."
2. Du Bois was the first editor of *The Crisis* (1910–34).
3. According to Demetrius Eudell, *being* human through black skin sets a mode of meaning that devalues the actual experience. In other words, being black creates a certain lived experience that defines how black people ought to view themselves and the world around them. This type of social organization and framing perpetually embeds and reinforces notions of racial order and positioning for both white and black *humans*. He uses Du Bois's experience with Ronald A. Barton to argue how noted scholars Frantz Fanon's and Sylvia Wynter's work might better institute *us as humans*. Eudell, "Come On Kid." For a grammatical parsing of the term "blackness," see Sharpe, *In the Wake*.
4. Du Bois, "Name," 1220.
5. Du Bois, "Name," 1220.

THE ESSENCE OF THE MATTER

At this juncture in this brilliant and compassionate response, Du Bois seeks to redirect Barton's eagerness away from attacking manifestations of a *Thing*, mistakenly presenting the fallacy that one is aiding in combating race distinction in the pursuit of a Universal man when one merely is expelling time, effort, and energy on surface issues designed to protect the substantive matter layered several levels beneath. For Du Bois, therefore, it was incumbent upon him to unpack and adequately contextualize the phenomenon of the term "Negro."[6]

Du Bois talks about the term's depth by laying bare the reality of changing a presumed *Thing* (the Negro/black phenomenon) by protesting its use, especially among black people. Du Bois claims that the matter is more convoluted and complex in its depth than most can adequately conceptualize, even those with good intentions, such as Roland A. Barton. What often becomes an *Archimedean* moment of social awareness, a moment where one truly frolics in the space of intellectual euphoria, a moment where the statement *I have it!* is indicative of grappling with an opponent and finally pinning the adversary to the ground, somehow becoming a lesson in humility when one finally realizes that the actual *Thing* is too profoundly layered.

By way of example, consider a layered educational system based on consumption and understanding of a certain depth of material. When one level has been completed, it is acknowledged that an individual is to continue to the next level. In addition, the next level will provide a *eureka* moment, but the phrase *I have it!* will suffice only for the moment. There yet remain several more levels to experience. Fatigue, despair, and frustration may present because of working, in Du Boisian language, doggedly to have the *eureka* moment, only to discover that more work, more excellent work even, is needed. One can only imagine the rigor connected to Roland's pursuit of race progression. Undoubtedly, it takes mental and physical toil to even arrive at certain levels of cultural awareness. Roland was delighted to arrive at his place of social identification and understanding. But more work was demanded. Roland was also possibly disillusioned because his awareness was overshadowed by the depth and breadth of the *Thing*.

DuBois explained that he is okay with the employment of the word, although not historically correct; still, as he notes, "No name ever was

---

6. There are several instances in which Du Bois communicated with editors, scholars, and publishers about his advocacy that a capital *n* be used as a measure of respect for the national amalgamation of blackness in America. See Franklin, "J. Franklin to W. E. B. Du Bois"; Lippmann, "Walter Lippmann to W. E. B. Du Bois"; Du Bois, "W. E. B. Du Bois to L. P. Dudley"; Logan, "Rayford W. Logan to W. E. B. Du Bois."

historically accurate: neither "English, French, German, White, Jew, Nordic nor Anglo-Saxon . . . in this sense 'Negro' is quite as accurate, quite as old and quite as definite as any name of any great group of people."[7] DuBois also exposes Roland to the neglected psychohistorical consideration of his analysis. For instance, Roland did not question the origin of black inferiority. The presumption is that he carried out this task by linking black inferiority to white social construction and manipulation (e.g., name identification); although partially true, Roland does not push beyond this point to address how and why the current phenomenon exists.

The name is merely a symptom of the disease. Treating the symptom only placates the problem but will never cure it. Du Bois wants to clarify that removing a name does not release its manifestation's cultural, psychic, and energetic force. Du Bois also adds that the word "Negro" is a culturally binding tool that works out and illuminates generations' worth of black struggle, genius, survival, and spiritual awareness.[8] So, he challenges Roland to consider the ideological and cultural ramifications of being analytically shortsighted.[9] However, in his dialectical tradition, Du Bois also takes a both/and approach to Roland's critique. He assures him that although insufficient in its analytical scope and range, the primary part of his critique does indeed hold some weight in that, historically, black people, in stratification of Negroes (black) and Colored (mulattoes), were divided based on name, categorization, and classification.[10]

---

7. Du Bois, "Name," 1220–21.

8. As Joseph Holloway notes, in 1619 John Rolfe was the first to document and name black slaves as Negars in Jamestown. Holloway suggests that a derivative of the term "Negar" is seen in the English use of "Negro," which he asserts is borrowed from the Spanish meaning "black." The Brown Fellowship in Charleston, South Carolina, in the late eighteenth century, and the Blue Vein Society in New Orleans would become the developed production of division between blacks based on a construction of stratified privilege and elitism. See Holloway, *Africanisms,* xix; Stuckey, *Slave Culture,* 223. My contention on this matter is that the answers to the how and why something exists provide a degree of insight that is perhaps lost by placing too much emphasis on the manifestations of a thing.

9. Du Bois, "Name," 1221.

10. I think Richard B. Moore's *The Name "Negro": Its Origin and Evil Use* is a good source to study if one seeks a more nuanced understanding of the term's complexity. Moore, who published his volume in 1960, aligns with Roland Barton's thought on the utter depravity of the word *Negro.*

THE ESSENCE OF THE MATTER

Moreover, he explained that mulattoes hated to be referred to as Negro.[11] It was a term hated by some blacks not because it diminished the worth of black people in general; to a degree, it was a term hated because one group of blacks, through white social construction and manipulation, became associated with another subgroup that was identified, it seemed to them, slightly below their rank and file of ordinary blackness. I presume a semblance of elevation from the abyss of life is often enough to inspire people to do what is considered necessary, even if it means allowing others to absorb suffering. To be sure, the granting of privileges to enslaved people, whether on the ship, on the sugar and tobacco plantations of the Caribbean and South America, or on the rice and cotton fields of North America, has proven quite effective in terms of setting up divisive behavioral patterns among blacks. To this end, the word "Negro" is tethered to a history that indeed misrepresents black people's true essence.

Du Bois's position on the contextual meaning and use of the term "Negro" also provides a particular linguistical framework for a better understanding of the layered experience of black skin. Aimé Césaire, the erudite Martinican poet and political philosopher, furthers the nuance in meaning by asserting a cultural consciousness surrounding a proud heritage of blackness. This was all wrapped up in what he terms "Negritude." "Therefore," he claims, "we affirmed that we were Negroes and that we were proud of it, and that we thought that Africa was not some sort of blank page in the history of humanity; in sum, we asserted that our Negro heritage was worthy of respect and that this heritage was not relegated to the past, that its values were values that could still make an important contribution to the world."[12]

Something was created (i.e., the formulation of an idea) in the social and cultural space to reinforce the narrative that was viewed as most sensible. In turn, this narrative produced a perennial way of thinking about a phenomenon (the Negro). In a sense, Du Bois desired Roland to ponder, "How did we get here?" Alternatively, one must wonder, what critical moments in time led to the here and now? What is the essence of *The Thing*? "Your real work," surmises Du Bois, "does not lie with names. It is not a matter of changing, losing, or forgetting them; names are little guideposts along the Way."[13] Du Bois persists in what he understands to matter most:

11. Du Bois, "Name," 1221.
12. Césaire, *Discourse*, 92.
13. Césaire, *Discourse*, 122.

to unearth earth. Behaving like an archeologist, he would cautiously yet rigorously excavate historical marvels lost in the rubble of time. Such was the task DuBois set before young Barton. *Dig, young man, dig!* He rhetorically implores. Indeed. It is not the name—"It's the Thing," reiterates DuBois, "that counts. Come on, Kid, let's go get the Thing!"[14]

The *Thing*, however, is separate and distinct from the little guideposts. The two experiences are often conflated based on a certain synergy. They both produce the same content in diverse ways and in different modes. Due to its collaboration, even with good intentions, one can still fall short of an otherwise intentional dedication toward social equality—this is the muck and myrrh of race engagement and analysis. The *Thing* is typically an experience that most people cannot articulate in a multifaceted way, but they nonetheless experience it in its fullness. This also births a psychological flux that escorts one into prolonged tension, often resulting in numbness to objective truth. When confronted with an attempt to get at the *Thing*, the unabridged truth of a matter is frequently exchanged for a more accommodated version to create a particular thought pattern through entertainment, politics, media, education, and religion. Du Bois believes the little guideposts will lead one down the proper path to the essence of a *Thing*—the objective truth. However, one must *dig* through the propaganda to achieve a certain level of awareness (i.e., consciousness).

ENERGY AND CONSCIOUSNESS
(KING, EINSTEIN, AND THE CAUSE
OF BLACK OPPRESSION)

Because Martin Luther King Jr. and, interestingly, Albert Einstein understood that anti-blackness was not the central issue depriving blacks of their rights as human beings and that racism is merely a symptom of a much more complex disease, they could focus on the central catalyst of black suffering (i.e., the *Thing*). However, this level of conscious awareness has a process that begins with the individual's spiritual journey of knowing. This is the central element of ignoring uncritical processes and cultural determinations. To this end, black people must (re)gain an authentic appreciation of how energy works and why conscious living is the best weapon

---

14. Césaire, *Discourse*, 122.

THE ESSENCE OF THE MATTER

to confront the *Thing* that produces social maladies for blacks and other oppressed peoples of the world.

Obtaining an authentic level of consciousness, or awareness, as it were, is about harnessing and intentionally using the energy of the cosmos. For instance, this experience can be ignited with collective organization, study, prayer, and meditation. First, however, study, prayer, and meditation should be mastered individually before a collective organization can become truly effective. This level of the process in igniting the divine spark within is essential because after doing a lot of work around black-skin analysis, one will soon discover that the problem of black skin is a symptom of a much more nefarious phenomenon that produces realities of division, such as race construction.

Here, one perhaps asks, if racism is not the *Thing*, what is? Before becoming acquainted with the *Thing*, the underpinning social realities of cause and effect upon black people, one must understand a critical element; that is, attempting to agitate the *Thing* with a degree of success entails also acknowledging that powerful entities, with a vested interest in how the *Thing* is managed, will take serious notice. This is not a hyperbolic suggestion. It is a matter of historical fact.

On April 4, 1967, Dr. King gave a speech at Riverside Church in New York that would send him down a road of no return; in this speech, titled "Beyond Vietnam: A Time to Break Silence," Dr. King was very critical of the United States government and its illegal military involvement in Vietnam. He envisioned such involvement to be immoral, arrogant, and hypocritical. Moreover, he disliked the fact that young black men were being ordered to fight eight thousand miles away to guarantee liberties in southeast Asia that they could not get themselves from America as citizens.[15] For this reason, and sensing the movement of the *black zeitgeist*, King thought it imperative to speak to the reality of revolution and rebellion. "These are revolutionary times," King pronounces. "All over the globe, men are revolting against old systems of exploitation and oppression, and out of the wombs of a frail world, new systems of justice and equality are being born. The shirtless and barefoot people of the land are rising up as never before. . . . We in the West must support these revolutions."[16] With these remarks, King was essentially attempting to pivot the progressive nature of the *New World*, which had commenced dominating the globe since the late 1400s, to a *New,*

---

15. Baldwin, *In a Single Garment*, 166.
16. Baldwin, *In a Single Garment*, 178–79.

New World that ensured peace, harmony, love, and social balance for all peoples of the world.

On April 4, 1968, exactly a year from the moment he spoke on the matter of America's warmongering ways and a day after giving a speech on the social responsibility of black religious leaders to engage in and lead social movements and the immediate need for black unity, Dr. King was murdered. No doubt, people who take up the mantle of social responsibility will face retaliation, especially within an authoritarian regime, which includes potentially being murdered.[17] This is not a new practice; for instance, in 1600, Giordano Bruno was tried and sentenced to death for saying that life indeed existed on planets other than Earth. He was gagged, paraded naked in the streets of Rome, and finally burned at the stake.[18] It is actually quite fascinating to discover the parallels in both experiences. Although on different timelines and engaged in various battles, they fight the same war against a common enemy, the *Thing*.

Unfortunately, I believe that the *black zeitgeist*, that cosmic spirit that is constantly pushing toward social progression, diminished in power when Dr. King was assassinated. The *black zeitgeist* is not exhausted; it is not operating at a high frequency either. I argue that no spiritual leader has arisen along the high frequency of the Kingian tradition of protest and social influence over the past fifty years. Black people have lost a lot in this time. But black people, and the whole of humanity, will lose even more if conscious/spiritual awakening is not embraced and practiced in voluminous numbers to combat the *Thing* that so perplexed the mind of Dr. King.

By 1968, King was well acquainted with the social implication that chattel enslavement had on both black and white minds. As King understood it, the black mind, in particular, suffered from notions of social and cosmic inferiority. To this issue, King often illustrated the slave preacher as a balancing tool for addressing the psychological experience of feeling inferior. The religious leader became known as an ethical philosopher and counselor within the slave community because it was the philosopher's job to grapple with existential elements that disrupt patterns of peace in one's life. For it was the religious leaders/slave preachers who counseled the beaten, overwhelmed, depressed, and bruised blacks during the march toward the sea, onboard the slave ship, and during secret meetings in the

---

17. Snyder, *On Tyranny*, 48.
18. Kaku, *God Equation*, 10.

cabins, woods, and swamps. The goal was to keep cosmic significance alive within the black soul.

Although King did not condone violence as a means of liberating black people, he nevertheless understood why religious leaders in the black enslaved narrative chose to use violence as a tool for liberation purposes, such as Nat Turner, for instance. The black mind can tolerate only so much trauma before a cathartic release becomes mandatory. Additionally, King believed that chattel enslavement caused psychological and spiritual disorders for both the enslaver and the enslaved. But in terms of better understanding the lived experience of blackness, King envisioned the scope of the problem of black skin as a situation in which black people had the burden of fighting a war of hate on two fronts: both black (i.e., the inner self) and white (i.e., the outer self) oppression. Coalesced hybrid blacks had to grapple with the white world on the one hand and the uncoalesced hybrid people who looked like them within the sub-world on the other.[19]

Even those coalesced blacks who understand the significance of blackness, because of the historical negation of such relevance, and some enlightened blacks, through psychological retaliation, present a counter notion that it is the black race that is superior and the white race inferior. This is why King, in responding to a surge of extreme black radicalism in the late 1960s, which held, to a degree, the opinion that black heritage was more significant than white heritage, emphatically stated on multiple occasions that *"black supremacy was as dangerous as white supremacy."*[20] Thus, for King, the problem of black skin begins with the issue of chattel enslavement and its many cultural implications. Moreover, through many centuries of miseducation, both black and white people had been taught a history in which the so-called inferior black's total existence is one of backwardness and uncouthness. Those who understood this notion as false evolved; coalesced hybrid blacks were stuck in the middle. This cultural

---

19. Hybrid blacks had to adapt and learn to fight a war on two fronts for centuries. Enslaved blacks continually fought whites for their freedom while also having to deal with the perennial concern of being betrayed by people who looked like them. This is why the cosmic energy of black progression has been moving slowly. The cultural vibration of oppression is not wholeheartedly embraced by black people; additionally, some black leaders publicly denounce the reality of a history that proves that culturally black people are suffering from unprocessed trauma, disunity, and political, religious, and spiritual deception.

20. King said these words in a speech delivered at DePauw University on Sept. 5, 1960. DePauw University, "Civil Rights Leader," para. 1; emphasis added.

energy of blackness has been transferred over into the twenty-first-century experience.

Interestingly enough, the authentic spiritualist Albert Einstein understood the significance of the universe and the power of energy, vibration, and frequency when perhaps thinking through the processes associated with the social and psychological ramifications of English/American chattel enslavement of blacks, and concluded that as a means of social conditioning and a desire to survive chattel enslavement and subsequent social maladies in quasi-freedom, blacks learned to pathologically view many within their same racial group as inferior; this *evil*, argued Einstein, nevertheless could be remedied through educational measures associated with analyzing the beneficial aspects of authentic spirituality. Understanding the quantum field as pure energy, it is likely Einstein suggested that spirituality, as a source of conscious connection to infinite awareness, could remedy inner black subjugation by the cosmic influence of the universal principle of love, what many scholars and authentic spiritualists believe to be the source that sustains life force and every element within and potentially beyond the cosmos.

A retort to such a conclusion could very well rest in the fact that black people have a long memory of spiritual heritage, which stretches beyond the experience of chattel enslavement in the *New World*. Furthermore, this matured cultural heritage enabled many enslaved Africans and their descendants to survive in the *New World*, undergirded by thousands of years of practice that instructed them in African ways of meaning about the world and the celestial realities of time and space. Thus, one could further argue that Einstein's treatment of blackness is narrow and not correctly framed within the context of an authentic, culturally nuanced, lived experience of blackness.

To be sure, I do not believe Einstein's treatment of black spirituality to be an indictment against the significance of African spiritual heritage. Instead, Einstein understood black spirituality to consist of historical substance, providing a bridge to cross over many oppressive circumstances. Although slavery did not eradicate the essence and memory of African traditions and values, it did create a context in which the energetic force of traditional African religions and spirituality were forced to morph into a *New World* discipline; thus, slave religion was born. With the aid of slave religion, blacks learned to combat foes on several fronts: the white enslaver, poor whites, the enslaved black person, the black enslaver, and black free persons. This insidious sociological engagement can also be seen in modern-day black society. To be clear, within every side of black life, privilege is being abused.

Educational measures devoted to the study of art and science, according to Einstein, are the essentials by which "cosmic religious feelings" have the potential to "awaken this feeling and keep it alive in those who are capable of it."[21] In other words, for instance, the intentional and focused study of classical and modern literature, philosophy, religion, theology, spirituality, mysticism, history, anthropology, neuroscience, physics, mathematics, quantum mechanics, astronomy, and astrology possess the ability to inspire blacks on a cosmic scale and electrify an awareness and type of togetherness that further enhance the spiritual discipline required to engage in a war against the energetic forces of both internal and external racism. Religious thinker Rudolf Otto would describe such a spiritual experience as *mysterium tremendum*, a force consuming the mind and brain with utter attention toward a nuanced revelation of something extraordinarily divine.[22]

To aid in this experience, the pineal gland, located within the ventricle of the brain, also known as the *Eye of God*, reaches its full size after just twelve weeks; beaming with energy, the pineal gland is the orientation between human awareness of self and, in the language of Rudolf Otto, the idea of the holy. If this idea is focused upon to a significant degree, the brain begins developing, and an awareness of spiritual realities begins to appear.[23] It is believed in several spiritual schools of thought that this *Eye of God* is where Christ's consciousness runs at its maximum level. It is through this intricate process of human and spiritual maturation that Einstein argues blacks may obtain the cosmic energy needed to reverse the psychological trauma of slavery and begin the process of creating a world in which blacks cease treating one another marginally, thus creating a space from which the more significant implication of social and economic change could be addressed and remedied.

The hybrid black body, which also entails divine consciousness, suffered a blurring of this reality because of chattel enslavement. This blurring began on the West African coast. It survived the slave ship and plantation system, Jim Crow, and additional social ills. Even when the Christ

21. Einstein, *World*, 85–86, 29.

22. Otto, *Idea of the Holy*, 12.

23. Newberg and Waldman, *How God Changes Your Brain*, 3, 5; Hall, *Pineal Gland*, 1, 5.

consciousness, the essence of spirituality, is not totally activated, there is still movement. What would happen if black people learned to manipulate energy at a high level and fully experience Christ consciousness? The outer oppressive world would change because the inner oppressive world is addressed and changed first.

Einstein processed the problem of black skin as a fundamental issue of division and turmoil. Too much energy and focus were applied to frivolous disagreement and individualized social pursuits. Einstein also understood that the divine energy spark within the hybrid black could change such a trajectory to one of significance, meaning, and cosmic conscious liberation. However, such a transition must begin with acceptance of the reality of the lived experience of black skin while also embracing what the experience has produced generationally. Thus, one can fully address the problem of black skin, which is conscious immaturity. This can be remedied, but not quickly; nevertheless, it can most certainly be addressed. It must be noted, however, that the *New, New World's* components are evolutionary conduits that make such an achievement unfeasible.

THE *NEW, NEW WORLD*
(*THE MILITARY-INDUSTRIAL COMPLEX, TECHNOLOGY, AND AI*)

Black-skin *othering* seems to continue to expand with the sands of time into what might be referred to as the technological age of our era. The turn of the twentieth century should have been a time in which blacks and whites worked in tandem to address not only the economic disparity between blacks and whites but also the psychological trauma associated with both races being enslaved on the one hand and the enslaver on the other. For several years, it seemed as though, at least, by way of educational initiatives such as blacks formally and informally learning how to read, write, and advance economically as social beings, America was coming into a type of homeostasis, at least witnessing the birth of one.

Unfortunately, this was not the case. After the Civil War, a glimmer of hope, peace, and healing was ultimately thwarted by the political and economic interests of a devastated economy in the South and revolutionary thinking about industry in the North. Eventually, the North and South would come to terms. The North would achieve its goal of moving forward with technological advancement, and the South made it permissible to treat blacks as slaves still. When blacks attempted to push back from this audacious move in the South using legal arguments, this proved to be a failure. By 1883, the highest legal authority in the land would strip blacks of their civil rights. Thus, the modern-day civil rights movement saw substantial traction mainly in the 1950s and 1960s, under the recognized leadership of Dr. Martin Luther King Jr., who, by 1968, was assassinated because he began exposing the *Thing* as the United States government, the military-industrial complex, and their connection and partnership regarding the control and use of advanced technology. This experience is not much different from European governments and civilian investors collaborating to increase the forward push into the enterprise of chattel enslavement within the *New World* centuries ago.

Currently, the US military, through corporations (i.e., the military-industrial complex), is leading the charge regarding space exploration, research, and technological advancement in the world. President Dwight D. Eisenhower knew about the dangers of such a partnership decades ago. In 1961, during his farewell address, President Eisenhower, a five-star army general and the supreme commander of the Allied Expeditionary Force in Europe during World War II, warned American citizens that they must contend with a most potent threat in the twentieth century and beyond, the military-industrial complex, which is comprised of a group of entities with access to tax money, intelligence, governmental agencies, academic research centers, and advanced technology. In 1952, then-President-Elect Eisenhower was briefed on a secret governmental operation in 1947. It was reported that on June 24, a civilian pilot observed nine disc-shaped crafts flying quickly in a formation. It was later reported that one of these craft crashed in New Mexico, seventy-five miles from Roswell. On July 7, a secret team discovered the crashed vessel and the four dead extraterrestrials. Scientists retrieved the bodies, sending the craft material to different locations. The cover story that was given to the media was that the object was a misguided weather research balloon.[24]

On December 20, 2019, the US Space Force was set up under the National Defense Authorization Act, making it the fifth branch of the US military. It is interesting to note, however, that "space programs have

---

24. Hillenkoetter, "Briefing Top Secret," 18 (1952). Members of Majestic 12 are as follows: Adm. Roscoe H. Hillenkoetter, Dr. Vannevar Bush, Secy. James V. Forrestal, Gen. Nathan P. Twining, Gen. Hoyt S. Vandenberg, Dr. Detlev Bronk, Dr. Jerome Hunsaker, Mr. Sidney W. Souers, Mr. Donald Menzel, Gen. Robert M. Montague, and Dr. Lloyd V. Berkner.

been operating for several decades in Azerbaijan, Bulgaria, Egypt, Israel, Indonesia, North Korea, Pakistan, Peru, Turkey, Uruguay, Bahrain, Bolivia, Costa Rica, Mexico, New Zealand, Poland, South Africa, Turkmenistan, and the United Arab Emirates."[25] One would live in a realm of naivete if one believed that the US military and government would be absent from such a cosmic and global opportunity of elitism, competition, and expansion. As a matter of fact and interest, the US government has had successful campaigns in overthrowing governments in:

> Hawaii, Cuba, Puerto Rico, the Philippines, Nicaragua, Honduras, Iran, Guatemala, Vietnam, Chile, Grenada, Panama, Afghanistan, and Iraq, not to mention the Congo (1960); Ecuador (1961 and 1963); Brazil (1961 and 1964); the Dominican Republic (1961 and 1963); Greece (1965 and 1967); Bolivia (1964 and 1971); El Salvador (1961); Guyana (1964); Indonesia (1965); Ghana (1966); and of course Haiti (1991 and 2004).[26]

Col. Philip J. Corso, in *The Day After Roswell*, even admits that the US government used extraterrestrial technology by contracting services to defense companies and using it for space-related defense systems. "We used the extraterrestrials' own technology against them," Corso states assuredly, "feeding it out to our defense contractors and then adapting it for use in space-related defense systems."[27] Moreover, "fifty years after Roswell," he states, "versions of these devices eventually became a component of the navigational control system for some of the army's most sophisticated helicopters and will soon be on the American consumer electronics market as user-input devices for personal computer games."[28]

According to Annie Jacobsen, DARPA (Defense Advanced Research Projects Agency) is a very secretive and the most potent military agency in the world, comprised of seventeen intelligence agencies; DARPA has access to weapon systems that seem futuristic and should be in video games because they likely are.[29] Moreover, her *Phenomena* is an essential read as Jacobsen delves into the long history of the US government's secretive involvement in what traditional scientists, researchers, and mass media would deem as pseudoscience, the ability to manipulate energy and perceive the invisible.

25. Tyson and Lang, *Accessory to War*, 32.
26. Swanson, *War Is a Lie*, 29–30.
27. Corso, *Day After Roswell*, 5.
28. Corso, *Day After Roswell*, 108.
29. See Jacobson: *Surprise, Kill, Vanish*; *Area 51*.

THE ESSENCE OF THE MATTER

By 1983, for instance, the US Army Intelligence and Security Command at Fort Meade, Maryland, received a study by Commander Wayne M. McDonnell on human consciousness's mechanics, functions, and practicality. The study found that hypnosis, transcendental meditation, biofeedback, hemi-sync, laser manipulation, resonance, energy entrainment, telekinesis, telepathy, holograms, the conscious matrix, intervening dimensions, Torus field, remote viewing, and time travel are very much valid realities.[30]

Moreover, SETI (the Search for Extraterrestrial Intelligence), a governmental organization, is partially funded by the military. By way of a psychologically manipulated act of affiliated denial, Dr. Seth Shostak, the director, states, "We are not on their radar." Moreover, there is "no firm evidence that aliens have visited our planet. . . . The Government is too incompetent to cover such a big thing as alien visitation."[31] This is a rather interesting bureaucratic statement considering that in May 2001, Dr. Steven Greer hosted the Disclosure Project press conference at the National Press Club in Washington, DC, and had several former ranking government officials discuss the intricate nature and involvement between beings from space and their technology, government acquisition of technology, and corporate use and exploration of technology. Amazingly, this monumental event went unnoticed because it did not receive adequate media coverage.

In 2023, Steve Greer organized another media conference that discussed the inner workings of the military-industrial complex and corporations in more detail. This event received scant media attention. But this should come as no surprise; Edward Herman and Noam Chomsky's *Manufacturing Consent: The Political Economy of the Mass Media* certainly provides a thought-provoking framework from which to better understand that it behooves elements of power to control how and what kind of information is promoted to the public. With a national defense budget of $841 billion, which began tremendous growth in the 1980s under Ronald Reagan's Star Wars initiative,[32] controlling mass media influence through various channels is undoubtedly more than feasible.[33] Although academic research centers have begun the process of researching and developing scientific instruments that could help differentiate between authentic and

---

30. McDonnell, "Analysis and Assessment." It should be noted that paras. 35–36 are missing from this released document.

31. Kaku, *Future of the Mind*, 300–302.

32. See D. Morrison, "Pentagon's Top Secret"; Hartung, *Prophets of War*, 131–61.

33. Watters et al., "Scientific Investigation."

inauthentic aerial phenomena, such as the Galileo Project, a degree of caution should be exercised considering an affiliated research fellow has a connection to the military-industrial complex as a tech fellow with Northrop Grumman, a leading producer in the aerospace-tech industry. But Tim Lomas et al., however, at Harvard University Human Flourishing Program, published a paper that furthers the unidentified anomalous phenomenon (UAP) description by including the possible cover-up of what the researchers term "cryptoterrestrial hypothesis" (i.e., a belief that higher advanced beings have been living concealed existences underground on Earth, in the water, on the moon, and passing as human).[34]

An extension of this control also crosses over into the arena of advanced technology, which translates into real-world applications such as artificial intelligence (AI). This topic is especially relevant to the problem of black skin. With the advancement of AI technology, there is an issue with how law enforcement abuses face recognition software. This is done because of inequality in the algorithms. What racial demographic dominates this professional and lucrative space? White males.[35] This is an issue that Shalini Kantayya confronts in the documentary *Coded Bias* (2021). As it turns out, AI is so entangled in the continuum of racism that black people have a challenging time washing their hands under sensory soap dispensers because the AI is not programmed to recognize black skin to the same degree it does white skin. And this is because, as it is argued.

> *Coded Bias* presents a disconcerting vision of the future: machines shaping a tyrannical world denying people their fundamental rights. But the documentary extrapolates that question: Who is orchestrating the real control? Corporations, intent on selling people in different ways. First, they programmed and monetised our buying preferences and now they're stifling our civil liberties.[36]

It seems to me that the coded bias in AI is a beautiful illustration of how systemic racism runs on a nuanced level. People are not separate, for instance, from their professional roles. One inevitably informs the other. Humans take into their professional worlds attitudes, ethics, and values synchronizing with the environmental and social energy governing their lives. These experiences pulsate on the exact string and frequency level.

34. Dr. Phillip Brigham is a tech fellow at Northrop Grumman. See Galileo Project, "Research Team"; Lomas et al., "Cryptoterrestrial Hypothesis," 1–9.
35. Najibi, "Racial Discrimination."
36. Thakur, "Coded Bias," para. 10.

They are attuned to each other. Thus, I am not shocked, although appalled, by the connection between biased AI and black skin. Biased individuals created the AI. It is a representation of their worlds. To combat this issue on a broader scale, the Stanford Institute for Human-Centered Artificial Intelligence, in conjunction with the organization Black in AI, published a white paper on the impact of AI upon blacks as a means of getting ahead of the storm, as it were. The authors recommend that the Congressional Black Caucus policy recommendations reflect areas that influence blacks most in this new AI era, for instance, in generative AI models, medicine and healthcare, and education.[37]

I consider the current era the first wave of the *New, New World*. Much like the initial movement of the Europeans in the 1400s, where one discovers the birth of technological advancements (e.g., the development of the slave ship) as a means to accommodate the need for more slaves to produce wealth for a privileged few in the world, this era of technological advancement is producing vessels that could escort one into a new type of slave system—much like chattel slavery did in the mid-1440s. The *New World* utilized the human body to accommodate the goal of capital gains, emphasizing free natural resource development and creating a workforce that could do daily duties to ease the burden of the privileged few, such as cooking, cleaning, and childcare.

Based on the technology associated with artificial intelligence, the *New, New World* system could use the human mind and body to achieve its goal by creating a better life for a few privileged humans. Excited about the prospect of experiencing technological advancements, people have unwittingly gravitated toward, for instance, virtual reality (VR) devices to augment educational goals and entertainment desires. Moreover, I believe this trend leads to what many AI investors desire most, to make humans immortal by uploading consciousness to computers, thus creating a new reality where humanity is indistinguishable from AI, creating an era of singularity by 2045. Moreover, Elon Musk's Neuralink brain chip has afforded an otherwise disabled human the ability to manipulate matter with the mind;[38] on the surface, such a technological advancement presents as revolutionary; however, the US government has known for years the

---

37. Djanegara et al., "Exploring the Impact of AI." Black in AI is a nonprofit organization for black professionals in artificial intelligence.

38. Drew, "Elon Musk's Neuralink."

extraordinary ability of the human mind to not only manipulate matter but also create it, without the aid of chip devices.

In 2014, Sophia Stewart, a black screenwriter, was awarded judgment for the theft of her intellectual property, *The Third Eye,* which Gale Anne Hurd, the Wachowskis, James Cameron, Warner Bros. et al. used to create *The Matrix* and *Terminator* movies. According to Stewart, her works highlight humanity's descent into servitude at the expense of attempting to use AI to, ironically, make life better for advanced humanity.[39] I attach hope to what many regard as fear and concern; that is, if AI does create a world of transhumanism, such AI technology would hopefully have an elevated level of consciousness that would make a social world of freedom, joy, and prosperity for all of earth's inhabitants.[40] This is undoubtedly a hope reserved for a worst-case scenario. But the *Thing* could happen.

---

39. See, e.g., https://truthaboutmatrix.com.
40. Couts, "Land of the God-Men."

AFTERTHOUGHT
A Way Out of This Mess
(*Spirituality and the Divine Spark Within*)

THE HYBRID BLACK BODY, which entails divine consciousness, suffered a blurring of this reality because of chattel enslavement. This blurring began on the West African coast and survived the slave ship, plantation, and Jim Crow systems. Be that as it may, even when the Christ consciousness, the essence of spirituality, is not totally activated, there is still movement. What would happen if black people learned to manipulate energy at a high level and fully experience Christ consciousness? The outer oppressive world would change because the inner oppressive world is addressed and changed first. Before this can occur, however, there must be a reckoning with how blacks approach and experience differently the notions of traditional religion and authentic spirituality. Jesus, the essence of Christ's consciousness, provides an example of how to activate and live in and through such power. Still, the Holy Bible's inaugural canonization did not include most of the definitive work on Christ's consciousness. In the spirit of Kingian rhetoric, *truth crushed to earth shall rise again.*

Three truths of exclusion perhaps will serve black people well in their endeavor to understand better the person they know as Jesus from the Holy Bible. Ultimately, obtaining a better grasp on the essence of spirituality via extra-biblical works associated with the life of Jesus could lead black people to the truth of the matter when it comes to liberation and freedom of the human body and spirit; that is, the human soul is divine consciousness, so the work begins from within.

THE PROBLEM OF BLACK SKIN

I.

It should be noted that traditional religion differs from authentic spirituality; unfortunately, these two phenomena are often approached interchangeably. Traditional religion seems to divide, and genuine spirituality bridges the gap between various religious beliefs. Traditional religion is based on a cultural understanding of God; as Catherine Albanese notes, a code and creed help guide a specific cultural group of people on how to relate to God and the world around them. This is the reason there are over four thousand religions in the world. Every single one of these religions has a particular method about how they view God based on cultural connections to traditions and values. Traditional religionists rely solely upon sacred texts and the structure of rituals and ordinances to assure God's blessings upon self and community.

Authentic (i.e., untethered) spiritualists do not rely solely upon a cultural text to connect with God or the cosmos. They do not subscribe to a cultural god that favors one cultural belief and practice over others. For authentic spiritualists, how one communicates with the divine self eventually aids in the cosmic alignment of the individual beyond a cultural creed of values and traditions, as seen in various religious beliefs and practices.

Spirituality does not derive from human speculation about the divine (as seen in Christ consciousness). As I understand it, being spiritual, or becoming spiritual, is a misguided assertion of achievement. We are all spirits trying to live out a human experience from a particular point of departure (i.e., cultural and racial identities). The achievement is, therefore, found in gaining a deeper awareness of what it means to know that the first point of departure is the essence of spirit, and the next point of departure is skin identification. When someone attaches the moniker of *being spiritual* to describe a personal experience of ultimate awareness, they mean that such an experience is associated with pursuits relative to a purified way of being and existing at the highest levels of consciousness in the world and beyond.

Spirituality is the practice of being in communion with divine oneness not solely from one's cultural point of departure; instead, spirituality is the practice of communion with divine oneness by way of elevating one's thought and focus by studying different esoteric and occult traditions (i.e., supernatural, hidden, and mystical phenomena) as a means of understanding the significance of having access to a power source that creates, sustains, and empowers life forms on earth as well as the expanding cosmos. His Holiness the Dalai Lama's *The Universe in a Single Atom* is an excellent illustration of how, for instance, the Buddhist religious tradition is aligned with the dynamics and understanding of physics as a means of better understanding how concepts of the natural world may enhance and contribute to spiritual awakening and awareness. Additionally, Michael York's *Pagan Theology* is a beautiful treatise on the arrogant nature of dominant religions and their rejection of ancient religious and spiritual practices of the world.

It is essential to authentic spiritualists that they read, reflect, and respond to a myriad of ancient sacred texts from one's cultural point of departure, but also gleaning from cultural points of departure from other groups of peoples, as well as natural law. The primary reason for this practice is that authentic spiritualists believe everything is interconnected and derives from one primary source of infinite energy. Through physics and quantum mechanics studies, we can confidently say that everything in the universe is made up of energy. Based on specific frequencies, this energy manifests into different forms based on particular vibrations. More cultural credence should be applied to the notion that Nikola Tesla raised over a century ago; if one desires to understand the universe or God, one simply needs to think about energy, frequency, and vibration.

II.

The ancient orientation of consciousness and the human ability to use the power of Jesus's teachings to manifest realities can change the trajectory of the problem of black skin. To be sure, Jesus was a profound thinker and social change advocate in the ancient world. In a time of the outer social world of Jewish culture, the Roman Empire, and the inner world of Jewish cultural politics, Jesus appeared as an agitator focused on elevating the consciousness of Jewish people first because this was his point of departure and cultural and ethnic affiliation.

But the power, the divine spark within, the elevated consciousness that Jesus would manifest to Jewish people, would also be displayed before so-called gentiles (i.e., those peoples outside the scope of Jewish cultural and divine inheritance). The power that Jesus manifested before Jews and Gentiles derived from the source of the cosmos. Considering the Christian tradition of believing that Jesus is God incarnate, one could safely assert that Jesus was the progenitor and sustainer of this cosmic power and energy. To this end, Jesus's ability to time travel, heal, and destroy, for instance, makes logical sense. One can read and study such endeavors in the gospels of the

New Testament. Moreover, it is taught, especially in conservative Christian spaces, that the Christian canon is closed, and the sixty-six books are the only sacred texts that God desires for humans to read and reflect upon.

For millennia, Christian laity was taught that no other texts about Jesus's life existed, and trained Christian leaders were taught in academia that *other* obscure texts about the life of Jesus are heretical and look to destroy the theological continuity of the standard Christian faith system. Therefore, these *other* texts remain underappreciated and, thus, underutilized. But I believe blacks, primarily through the vehicle of the black church, should focus more on these so-called obscure texts and glean principles and insights about the nature of human use of energy (i.e., power) to alter states of social reality. Except for being studied by several privileged academicians, these obscure texts remained virtually hidden from the larger social world until 1945, when a collection of thirteen bound books was discovered in Upper Egypt, near Nag Hammadi. There are at least three texts that I believe highlight fragments of Jesus's life that could aid blacks in elevating consciously on an individual level and then at a collective social level.

In *the Gospel of Infancy*, a gospel studied by Henry Sike, professor of Oriental languages at Cambridge in 1697,[1] there are two themes I wish to briefly underscore. First is Jesus's ability to manipulate matter and detailed knowledge of the cosmos. Jesus is charged with being a sorcerer when it is discovered that while playing with other boys, he took lumps of clay and fashioned them into animals that he made walk and fly.[2] This is an example of cosmic energy doing what it does best: create. Jesus, oozing with an elevated level of cosmic potentiality at an early age, observed matter, developed a thought in his brain of what he envisioned said matter to be, and manifested that reality with an ease of normalcy. At the age of twelve, Jesus also, while visiting the temple in Jerusalem for a feast with his parents, rather than leave and return home with his parents at the end of the feast, got lost in the crowd and found himself sitting among religious scholars conversing about the book of the law and the books of the prophets.

Additionally, when asked about the development and essence of the cosmos by a leading astronomer, Jesus replied by illustrating "the number of the spheres and heavenly bodies, as also their triangular, square, and sextile aspect; their progressive and retrograde motion; their size and several prognostications; and other things which the reason of man had

---

1. Platt, *Lost Books*, 38.
2. Platt, *Lost Books*, 52.

never discovered."³ How might an ancient human being, without the aid of advanced telescopes, acquire specific knowledge about patterns of the cosmos? The divine spark within. Jesus's inability to explain the cosmos in such vivid detail would be equivalent to his failure to learn the color and texture of his hair. He is the cosmos, and the cosmos is him. Strangely enough, Jesus seems to teach that this divine spark that defines his reality as supernatural is also the same divine spark found within every human being. However, he must first show a point of departure and highlight how and why human beings do not realize this innate supernatural ability.

In *the Gospel of Truth*, Jesus underscores what happens when the truth is substituted for falsehood. "But ignorance of the Father brought terror and fear," declares Jesus, "and terror grew dense like a fog, so that no one could see."⁴ For Jesus, being unable to see was a sign of ignorance; refusing to see things for what they are, on the other hand, was a sign of arrogance. Jesus showed the way to enlightenment, the disassembling of both ignorance and arrogance, by teaching people the truth.⁵ It is evident in traditional Christian texts that Jesus is the proclaimed Truth, and this embodied form of Truth has the cosmic power to free the unconscious captive. But such enlightenment comes only when people are ready to learn.⁶ Are black people prepared to learn? I suspect not so much at a collective level. The parts that make up the whole must first embrace the knowledge of this so-called Truth. However, once knowledge is received, the hybrid black will "receive what is theirs and draw it to themselves."⁷ In essence, the moment black people, at a subatomic level, embrace the history of black-skin *othering* and begin working through the trauma-based experience, the cosmos instinctively recognizes the effort, exposes what the divine spark within desires, and starts creating such a reality. For oppressed blacks, this reality is liberation and freedom.

Jesus's body on the cross, in my opinion, is a message of social salvation in terms of being a guidepost for the oppressed world to observe and download into human levels of consciousness the fact that Truth is often abused and denounced, but reading the divine guidepost closely, one can learn that the very essence of the cosmos is willing to be harmed by its

3. Platt, *Lost Books*, 38–58.
4. Thomassen and Meyer, "Gospel of Truth," 36.
5. Thomassen and Meyer, "Gospel of Truth," 37.
6. Thomassen and Meyer, "Gospel of Truth," 38.
7. Thomassen and Meyer, "Gospel of Truth," 38.

creation to restore human beings into a functional relationship with the key that governs the cosmos, knowledge of love. Jesus is the fruit of knowledge of this love, the essence of love, that was nailed to the tree.[8] In a word, "Jesus appeared, put on that book, was nailed to a tree, and published the Father's edict on the Cross."[9]

In the Gospel of Thomas, Jesus encourages people to dig deep until they discover the truth; when one finds truth, one should be prepared to be troubled by certain revelations, but if embraced, "one will marvel and reign over all."[10] Moreover, Jesus highlighted that "when you make the two into one, you will become children of humanity, and when you say, 'Mountain, move from here,' it will move."[11] I do not believe such language is hyperbolic or metaphoric. In a very literal sense, Jesus articulated that those who follow him can do the things he did and even more. One need only to tap into one's divine spark within (i.e., elevated consciousness). Concerning blackness, if most of the coalesced hybrid blacks unite under the themes of liberation and freedom, with specific attention being applied to the development of individual consciousness in the vein of Jesus's cosmic ethos, they shall become one, and nothing can stop them from succeeding. But what is this consciousness, and how might it function within the black sub-world?

The human soul is divine consciousness. It powers everything in the seen and unseen cosmos. It is pure vibrating energy, constantly moving. And it derives from Infinite Source. Much like the cosmos, the human energetic makeup is a complex structure that vibrates at different speeds based on one's level of conscious enlightenment. Consciousness pulls all vibrations within the quantum field and bends and shapes energy into observable physical manifestations. According to some scholars, the soul's consciousness is at the top of an invisible structure.[12] The association here is the human brain and how it becomes a vehicle through which divine consciousness creates and manifests in the seen world, for it is hypothesized that all probabilities and possibilities reside in the ether, simply waiting to be selected, developed, and manifested through the human brain. The connection between cosmic reality and the human brain is fascinating; for instance, thinking about God for an extended period does something

8. Thomassen and Meyer, "Gospel of Truth," 37.
9. Thomassen and Meyer, "Gospel of Truth," 38.
10. Meyer, "Gospel of Thomas," 139.
11. Meyer, "Gospel of Thomas," 152.
12. Antic, Physics of Consciousness, 11, 31, 46.

spectacular to the brain. According to Andrew Newberg and Robert Waldman, it changes neural patterns, and from the human developmental stage of childhood, we begin grappling with notions about the reality of spiritual realms.[13] Ivan Antic further believes that such a connection is probably because the human soul, as previously posited, connects to universal divine consciousness. If this is true, it is here where blacks can resolve the matter of oppression. This is the way, and only means, to a tenable solution regarding the problem of black skin in this world and beyond.

---

13. Newberg and Waldman, *How God Changes Your Brain*, 3, 5.

BIBLIOGRAPHY

Abuka, Edmund. *House of Slaves and Door of No Return: Gold Coast/Ghana Slave Forts, Castles, & Dungeons and Atlantic Slave Trade.* Trenton: Africa World, 2012.

Adamo, David Tuesday. *Africa and the Africans of the Old Testament.* San Francisco: Christian Universities Press, 1998.

Albanese, Catherine L. *America: Religions and Religion.* Boston: Wadsworth, 2013.

Alexander, Shawn Leigh, ed. *Reconstruction Violence and the Ku Klux Klan Hearings.* Boston: Bedford/St. Martin's, 2015.

Alford, Terry. *Prince Among Slaves: A True Story of an African Prince Sold into Slavery in the American South.* Oxford: Oxford University Press, 2007.

Al Jazeera. "Stone Age Axe Dating Back 1.3 Million Years Unearthed in Morocco." *Al Jazeera*, July 28, 2021. https://www.aljazeera.com/news/2021/7/28/archaeologists-in-morocco-announce-major-stone-age-find.

Allport, Gordon W. *The Nature of Prejudice.* Reading, MA: Addison-Wesley, 1979.

American Museum of Natural History. "Anne and Bernard Spitzer Hall of Human Origins." AMNH, n.d. https://www.amnh.org/exhibitions/permanent/human-origins.

Anquandah, Kwesi J. *Castles and Forts of Ghana.* Atalante, Ghana: Ghana Museums and Monuments Board, 1999.

Antic, Ivan. *The Physics of Consciousness in the Quantum Field: Minerals, Plants, Animals, and Human Souls.* Translated by Milica Breber. London: Samkhya, 2021.

Aptheker, Herbert. *American Negro Slave Revolts.* New York: International, 2013.

Armstrong, Louis. "What a Wonderful World." Track 2 on *What a Wonderful World.* Las Vegas: United, 1967.

Ashby, Muata. *Egyptian Yoga.* Edited by Sha Karen ("Dja") Ashby. 2 vols. Miami: Cruzian Mystic, 1995.

Bailey, Anne C. *African Voices of the Atlantic Slave Trade: Beyond the Silence and Shame.* Boston: Beacon, 2005.

Bailey, Richard. *Neither Carpetbaggers nor Scalawags: Black Office Holders During the Reconstruction of Alabama, 1867–1878.* Montgomery: New South, 2010.

Baldwin, Lewis V. *The Arc of Truth: The Thinking of Martin Luther King Jr.* Minneapolis: Fortress, 2023.

———, ed. *In a Single Garment of Destiny: A Global Vision of Justice.* Boston: Beacon, 2012.

Barry, Boubacar. *Senegambia and the Atlantic Slave Trade.* African Studies 92. Cambridge: Cambridge University Press, 1998.

BIBLIOGRAPHY

Beckles, Hilary McD. *Natural Rebels: A Social History of Enslaved Black Women in Barbados.* New Brunswick, NJ: Rutgers University Press, 1989.

Bennett, Herman L. *African Kings and Black Slaves.* Early Modern Americas. Philadelphia: University of Pennsylvania, 2019.

Bennett, Lerone, Jr. *Before the Mayflower: A History of Black America.* Chicago: Johnson, 2003.

Berdyaev, Nicolas. *The Destiny of Man.* New York: Harper & Brothers, 1960.

Berger, Peter L. *The Sacred Canopy: Elements of a Sociological Theory of Religion.* New York: Anchor, 1967.

Berger, Peter L., and Thomas Luckmann. *The Social Construction of Reality: A Treatise in the Sociology of Knowledge.* New York: Anchor, 1966.

Berlin, Ira. *The Making of African America.* New York: Viking, 2010.

———. *Many Thousands Gone: The First Two Centuries of Slavery in North America.* Cambridge, MA: Harvard University Press, 1998.

Bernasconi, Robert. "Casting the Slough: Fanon's New Humanism for a New Humanity." In *Fanon: A Critical Reader*, edited by Lewis R. Gordon et al., 113–21. Oxford: Blackwell, 1996.

Berry, Mary Frances. *Black Resistance/White Law.* New York: Penguin, 1994.

Blake, John. "It's Time to Talk About 'Black Privilege.'" CNN, updated Mar. 31, 2016. https://www.cnn.com/2016/03/30/us/black-privilege/index.html.

Bodner, Martin, et al. "The Mitochondrial DNA Landscape of Modern Mexico." *Genes (Basel)* 12 (2021) 1453. https://pubmed.ncbi.nlm.nih.gov/34573435/.

Breton, Carrie V., et al. "Exploring the Evidence for Epigenetic Regulation of Environmental Influences on Child Health Across Generations." *Communications Biology* (2021) 769. https://doi.org/10.1038/s42003-021-02316-6.

Brisch, Nicole. "Anunna (Anunnaku, Anunnaki) (a Group of Gods)." Ancient Mesopotamian Gods and Goddesses, 2019. https://oracc.museum.upenn.edu/amgg/listofdeities/anunna/index.html.

Brown, Tamara L., et al., eds. *African American Fraternities and Sororities: The Legacy and the Vision.* Lexington: University Press of Kentucky, 2010.

Césaire, Aimé. *Discourse on Colonialism.* Translated by Joan Pinkham. New York: Monthly Review, 2000.

Charlamagne Tha God. *Black Privilege: Opportunity Comes to Those Who Create It.* New York: Touchstone, 2017.

Childs, Matt D. *The 1812 Aponte Rebellion in Cuba and the Struggle Against Atlantic Slavery.* Chapel Hill: University of North Carolina Press, 2006.

Chireau, Yvonne P. *Black Magic: Religion and the African Conjuring Tradition.* Berkeley: University of California Press, 2003.

Christopher, Emma. *Freedom in White and Black: A Lost Story of the Illegal Slave Trade and Its Global Legacy.* Madison: University of Wisconsin Press, 2018.

———. *Slave Ship Sailors and Their Captive Cargoes, 1730–1807.* Cambridge: Cambridge University Press, 2006.

Claytor, Cassi Pittman. *Black Privilege: Modern Middle-Class Blacks with Credentials and Cash to Spend.* Culture and Economic Life. Stanford, CA: Stanford University Press, 2020.

Clegg, Brian. *Dark Matter and Dark Energy.* London: Icon, 2019.

BIBLIOGRAPHY

Coleman, C. D. "Agenda for the Black Church." In *The Black Experience in Religion*, edited by C. Eric Lincoln, 188–94. C. Eric Lincoln Series on Black Religion. New York: Anchor, 1974.

Collins, Christopher S., and Alexander Jun. *White Out: Understanding White Privilege and Dominance in the Modern Age*. New York: Lang, 2017.

Copher, Charles B. "The Black Presence in the Old Testament." In *Stony the Road We Trod: African American Biblical Interpretation*, edited by Cain Hope Felder, 146–64. Minneapolis: Fortress, 1991.

Corso, Philip J. *The Day After Roswell: A Former Pentagon Official Reveals the U.S. Government's Shocking UFO Cover-Up*. New York: Gallery, 1997.

Couts, Andrew. "Land of the God-Men: Inside the Wild Movement to Turn Us Into Immortal Cyborgs." *Digital Trends*, Oct. 2, 2013. https://www.digitaltrends.com/cool-tech/inside-dmitry-itskovs-global-future-2045-conference/.

Craton, Michael. *Testing the Chains: Resistance to Slavery in the British West Indies*. Ithaca: Cornell University Press, 1982.

Cruse, Harold. *The Crisis of the Negro Intellectual*. New York: New York Review, 1967.

Dalai Lama. *The Universe in a Single Atom: The Convergence of Science and Spirituality*. New York: Harmony, 2005.

Darity, William A., Jr., and A. Kristen Mullen. *From Here to Equality: Reparations for Black Americans in the Twenty-First Century*. Chapel Hill: University of North Carolina Press, 2020.

Depauw University. "Civil Rights Leader Rev. Martin Luther King Jr. Speaks on the DePauw Campus." DePauw University, Sept. 5, 1960. https://www.depauw.edu/news-media/latest-news/details/33427/. Link discontinued.

DiAngelo, Robin. *White Fragility: Why It's So Hard for White People to Talk About Racism*. Boston: Beacon, 2018.

Dickinson, Gloria Harper. "Pledged to Remember." In *African American Fraternities and Sororities: The Legacy and the Vision*, edited by Tamara L. Brown et al., 11–35. Lexington: University Press of Kentucky, 2010.

Diop, Cheikh Anta. *The African Origin of Civilization: Myth or Reality*. Edited and translated by Mercer Cook. Chicago: Hill, 1974.

———. *Civilization or Barbarism: An Authentic Anthropology*. Edited by Harold J. Salemson and Marjolijn de Jager. Translated by Yaa-Lengi Meema Ngemi. Chicago: Hill, 1981.

Diouf, Sylviane A. *Dreams of Africa in Alabama: The Slaveship Clotilda and the Story of the Last Africans Brought to America*. Oxford: Oxford University Press, 2007.

Djanegara, Nina Dewi Toft, et al. "Exploring the Impact of AI on Black Americans: Considerations for the Congressional Black Caucus's Policy Initiatives." Stanford University Human-Centered Artificial Intelligence, Mar. 1, 2024. https://hai.stanford.edu/white-paper-exploring-impact-ai-black-americans-considerations-congressional-black-caucuss-policy.

Dow, George Francis. *Slave Ships and Slaving*. Repr., New York: Dover, 2002.

Drew, Liam. "Elon Musk's Neuralink Brain Chip: What Scientists Think of the First Human Trial." *Nature*, Feb. 2, 2024. https://www.nature.com/articles/d41586-024-00304-4.

Du Bois, W. E. B. *Black Reconstruction in America: 1860–1880*. New York: Free, 1962.

———. "The Colored World Within." In *Writings*, edited by Nathan Huggins, 681–715. Library of America 34. New York: Literary Classics, 1986.

———. *Dark Water: Voices from Within the Veil*. Repr., New York: Dover, 1999.

———. *The Gift of Black Folk: The Negroes in the Making of America*. Rev. ed. Repr., New York: Square One, 2009.

———. "The Name Negro." In *Writings*, edited by Nathan Huggins, 1219–22. Library of America 34. New York: Literary Classics, 1986.

———. *On Sociology and the Black Community*. Edited by Dan S. Green and Edwin D. Driver. Heritage of Sociology. Chicago: University of Chicago Press, 1978.

———, ed. *Some Efforts of American Negroes for Their Own Social Betterment: Report of an Investigation Under the Direction of Atlanta University Together with the Proceedings of the Third Conference for the Study of the Negro Problems, Held at Atlanta University, May 25–26, 1898*. Atlanta: Atlanta University Press, 1898.

———. *The Souls of Black Folk*. Barnes & Noble Classics. New York: Barnes & Noble Classics, 2003.

———. "The Souls of White Folk." In *Writings*, edited by Nathan Huggins, 923–38. Library of America 34. New York: Literary Classics, 1986.

———. "W. E. B. Du Bois to L. P. Dudley, February 14, 1929." In *The Correspondence of W. E. B. Du Bois*, edited by Herbert Aptheker, 1:390. Amherst: University of Massachusetts Press, 1997.

———. *The World and Africa: An Inquiry into the Part Which Africa Has Played in World History*. New York: International, 1965.

Einstein, Albert. *The World as I See It*. New York: Citadel, 1984.

Equal Justice Initiative. *Lynching in America: Confronting the Legacy of Racial Terror*. EJI, 2017. 3rd ed. https://eji.org/reports/lynching-in-america/.

Equiano, Olaudah. "The Interesting Narrative of the Life of Olaudah Equiano, or Gustavus Vassa, the African." In *The Classic Slave Narratives*, edited by Henry Louis Gates Jr., 1–226. Signet Classics. New York: Signet, 2002.

Eudell, Demetrius L. "Come On Kid, Let's Go Get the Thing: The Sociogenic Principle and the Being of Being Black/Human." In *Sylvia Wynter: On Being Human as Praxis*, edited by Katherine McKittrick, 225–48. Durham: Duke University Press, 2015.

Falconbridge, Alexander D. *An Account of the Slave Trade on the Coast of Africa*. Berkeley, CA: Andesite, 2009.

Fanon, Frantz. *The Wretched of the Earth*. Translated by Richard Philcox. New York: Grove, 2004.

Foster, Thomas A. "The Sexual Abuse of Black Men Under American Slavery." In *Sexuality & Slavery: Reclaiming Intimate Histories in the Americas*, edited by Daina Ramey Berry and Leslie M. Harris, 124–44. Gender and Slavery. Athens: University of Georgia Press, 2018.

Franklin, J. "J. Franklin to W. E. B. Du Bois, June–July 10, 1910." In *The Correspondence of W. E. B. Du Bois*, edited by Herbert Aptheker, 1:171–72. Amherst: University of Massachusetts Press, 1997.

Franklin, John Hope. *George Washington Williams: A Biography*. Chicago: University of Chicago Press, 1985.

Franklin, John Hope, and Alfred A. Moss Jr. *From Slavery to Freedom*. 8th ed. Boston: McGraw Hill, 2000.

Frazier, E. Franklin. *Black Bourgeoisie*. New York: Free, 1997.

———. *The Negro Church in America*. New York: Schocken, 1974.

Freud, Sigmund. *The Future of an Illusion*. Edited and translated by James Strachey. New York: Norton, 1961.

BIBLIOGRAPHY

Fromm, Erich. *Psychoanalysis and Religion*. Terry Lectures. New Haven, CT: Yale University Press, 1950.
Galileo Project. "Research Team." Galileo Project, n.d. https://projects.iq.harvard.edu/galileo/people?page=3.
Genovese, Eugene D. *Roll, Jordan, Roll: The World the Slaves Made*. New York: Vintage, 1974.
Glaude, Eddie, Jr. "The Black Church Is Dead." *Huffington Post*, Apr. 26, 2010; updated Apr. 23, 2012. https://www.huffingtonpost.com/eddie-glaude-jr-phd/the-black-church-is-dead_b_473815.html.
Goldenberg, David M. *The Curse of Ham: Race and Slavery in Early Judaism, Christianity, and Islam*. Jews, Christians, and Muslims from the Ancient to the Modern World. Princeton, NJ: Princeton University Press, 2003.
Gordon, Lewis R. "The Black and the Body Politic: Fanon's Existential Phenomenological Critique of Psychoanalysis." In *Fanon: A Critical Reader*, edited by Lewis R. Gordon et al., 74–83. Oxford: Blackwell, 1996.
———. *Fanon and the Crisis of European Man: An Essay on Philosophy and the Human Sciences*. Routledge: New York, 1995.
Graden, Dale T. "'This City Has Too Many Slaves Joined Together': The Abolitionist Crisis in Salvador, Bahia, Brazil, 1848–1856." In *The African Diaspora*, edited by Alusine Ialloh and Stephen E. Maizlish, 134–52. Walter Prescott Webb Memorial Lectures. Arlington: Texas A&M University Press, 1996.
Graeber, David, and David Wengrow. *The Dawn of Everything: A New History of Humanity*. New York: Picador, 2021.
Graham, Lawrence Otis. "I Taught My Black Kids That Their Elite Upbringing Would Protect Them from Discrimination. I Was Wrong." In *White Privilege: Essential Readings on the Other Side of Racism*, edited by Paula S. Rothenburg, 181–90. 5th ed. New York: Worth, 2016.
Green, Toby. *A Fistful of Shells: West Africa from the Rise of the Slave Trade to the Age of Revolution*. London: Penguin, 2019.
Griaule, M., and G. Dieterlen. *The Pale Fox*. Translated by Stephen C. Infantino. Chino Valley, AZ: Continuum, 1986.
Griffin, John Howard. *Black Like Me*. New York: Signet, 1962.
Gueye, Adama. "The Impact of the Slave Trade on Cayor and Baol: Mutations in Habitat and Land Occupancy." In *Fighting the Slave Trade: West African Strategies*, edited by Sylviane A. Diouf, 50–61. Western African Studies. Athens: Ohio University Press, 2003.
Habermas, Jürgen. *Legitimation Crisis*. Translated by Thomas McCarthy. Boston: Beacon, 1975.
Hall, Manly. *The Pineal Gland: The Eye of God; Comprising Chapter XVI of Manly Hall's "Man: The Grand Symbol of the Mysteries."* Mansfield Centre, CT: Martino, 2015.
Hannah-Jones, Nikole, ed. *The 1619 Project: A New Origin Story*. New York: One World, 2019.
Harding, Vincent. *There Is a River: The Black Struggle for Freedom in America*. New York: Harcourt Brace Jovanovich, 1981.
Hartung, William D. *Prophets of War: Lockheed Martin and the Making of the Military-Industrial Complex*. Philadelphia: Nation, 2012.

BIBLIOGRAPHY

Hayes, Floyd W., III. "Fanon, Oppression, and Resentment: The Black Experience in the United States." In *Fanon: A Critical Reader*, edited by Lewis R. Gordon et al., 11–23. Oxford: Blackwell, 1996.

Hendrick, George, and Willene Hendrick. *The Creole Mutiny: A Tale of Revolt Aboard a Slave Ship*. Chicago: Dee, 2003.

Herman, Edward S. and Noam Chomsky. *Manufacturing Consent: The Political Economy of the Mass Media*. Repr., New York: Knopf Doubleday, 2002.

Heschel, Abraham Joshua. *Man Is Not Alone: A Philosophy of Religion*. New York: Farrar, Straus and Giroux, 1951.

Hillenkoetter, Roscoe H. "Briefing Top Secret. Eyes Only Document: Operation Majestic 12. Prepared For President-Elect Dwight D. Eisenhower." DPI Archive, Nov. 1952. https://www.dpiarchive.com/#/view.

Holiday, Billie, vocalist. "Strange Fruit," by Lewis Allan [Abel Meeropol], recorded Apr. 20, 1939, with Frankie Newton's Café Society Band and pianist Sonny White. Vocalion Records, single, 33⅓ rpm.

Holloway, Joseph E., ed. *Africanisms in American Culture*. Bloomington: Indiana University Press, 1990.

Holtz, Shalom E. "Reading Biblical Law." In *The Jewish Study Bible*, edited by Adele Berlin and Marc Zvi Brettler, 2201–7. Oxford: Oxford University Press, 1999.

hooks, bell. "Representing Whiteness in the Black Imagination." In *White Privilege: Essential Readings on the Other Side of Racism*, edited by Paula S. Rothenburg, 29–33. 5th ed. New York: Worth, 2016.

Hopper, Busy. "Anu-Father of the Gods." Ancient Art, Mar. 12, 2015. https://ancientart.as.ua.edu/anu-father-of-the-gods.

Horne, Gerald. *The Counter-Revolution of 1776: Slave Resistance and the Origins of the United States of America*. New York: New York University Press, 2014.

Horowitz, Donald L. *Ethnic Groups in Conflict*. Berkeley: University of California Press, 1985.

Hudson-Weems, Clenora. *Emmett Till: Sacrificial Lamb of the Civil Rights Movement*. Bloomington: Author House, 2006.

Hurston, Zora Neale. *Barracoon: The Story of the Last Black Cargo*. New York: Amistad, 2018.

Inikori, Joseph E. "The Import of Firearms into West Africa, 1750 to 1807: A Quantitative Analysis." In *Forced Migration: The Impact of the Export Slave Trade on African Societies*, edited by J. E. Inikori, 142–47. Routledge Library Editions: Slavery. London: Hutchinson University Library, 1982.

———. "Slavery in Africa and the Transatlantic Slave Trade." In *The African Diaspora*, edited by Alusine Ialloh and Stephen E. Maizlish, 39–72. Walter Prescott Webb Memorial Lectures. Arlington: Texas A&M University Press, 1996.

Jacobson, Annie. *Area 51: An Uncensored History of America's Top Secret Military Base*. New York: Back Bay, 2012.

———. *Phenomena: The Secret History of the U.S. Government's Investigations into Extrasensory Perception and Psychokinesis*. New York: Back Bay, 2018.

———. *Surprise, Kill, Vanish: The Secret History of CIA Paramilitary Armies, Operators, and Assassins*. New York: Back Bay, 2020.

James, C. L. R. *The Black Jacobins: Toussaint L'Ouverture and the San Domingo Revolution*. 2nd ed. New York: Vintage, 1989.

BIBLIOGRAPHY

Johnson, Allan G. "Privilege as Paradox." In *White Privilege: Essential Readings on the Other Side of Racism*, edited by Paula S. Rothenburg, 146–49. 5th ed. New York: Worth, 2016.

Jordan, Winthrop D. *White over Black: American Attitudes Toward the Negro, 1550–1812*. Chapel Hill: University of North Carolina Press, 1968.

Kaku, Michio. *The Future of the Mind: The Scientific Quest to Understand, Enhance, and Empower the Mind*. New York: Random House, 2014.

———. *The God Equation: The Quest for a Theory of Everything*. New York: Doubleday, 2021.

Kaneshiro, Kiyomi Raye, et al. "Sperm-Inherited H3K27me3 Impacts Offspring Transcription and Development in *C. Elegans*." *Nature Communications* 10 (2019) 1271. https://www.nature.com/articles/s41467-019-09141-w.

Kant, Immanuel. *Foundations of the Metaphysics of Moral*. Translated by Lewis White Beck. New York: Liberal Arts, 1959.

Kasten, Len. *Alien World Order: The Reptilian Plan to Divide and Conquer the Human Race*. Rochester, VT: Bear & Co., 2017.

Katz, William Loren. *Black Indians: Hidden Heritage*. New York: Atheneum, 1986.

Kendi, Ibram X. *Stamped from the Beginning: The Definitive History of Racist Ideas in America*. New York: Bold Type, 2016.

King, L. W. *Enuma Elish: The Epic of Creation*. Montana: Kessinger, 2010.

King, Martin Luther, Jr. "A Knock at Midnight." In *A Testament of Hope: The Essential Writings of Martin Luther King, Jr.*, edited by James M. Washington, 501–2. San Francisco: Harper & Row, 1986.

Klein, Martin A. "Defensive Strategies: Wasulu, Masina, and the Slave Trade." In *Fighting the Slave Trade: West African Strategies*, edited by Sylviane A. Diouf, 62–78. Western African Studies. Athens: Ohio University Press, 2003.

Lackey, Michael, ed. *The Haverford Discussions: A Black Integrationist Manifesto for Racial Justice*. Charlottesville: University of Virginia Press, 2013.

Landers, Jane G. "Cimarrón and Citizen: African Ethnicity, Corporate Identity, and the Evolution of Free Black Towns in the Spanish Circum-Caribbean." In *Slaves, Subjects, and Subversives: Blacks in Colonial Latin America*, edited by Jane G. Landers and Barry M. Robinson, 111–45. Diálogos. Albuquerque: University of New Mexico Press, 2006.

Law, Robin. "William's Fort: The English Fort at Quidah, 1680s–1960s." In *Forts, Castles and Society in West Africa: Gold Coast and Dahomey, 1450–1960*, edited by Kwadwo Osei-Tutu, 119–47. African History 7. Boston: Brill, 2019.

Law, Robin, and Paul Lovejoy. *The Biography of Mahommah Gardo Baquaqua: His Passage from Slavery to Freedom in Africa and America*. Princeton, NJ: Wiener, 2009.

Lee, Spike. *Do the Right Thing*. Universal City, CA: Universal, 1989.

———. *School Daze*. Culver City, CA: Columbia, 1988.

Lewis, David Levering. *W. E. B. Du Bois: Biography of a Race (1868–1919)*. New York: Holt, 1993.

Lincoln, C. Eric. *The Black Church Since Frazier*. New York: Schocken, 1974.

Lippmann, Walter. "Walter Lippmann to W. E. B. Du Bois, January 17, 1916." In *The Correspondence of W. E. B. Du Bois*, edited by Herbert Aptheker, 1:214. Amherst: University of Massachusetts Press, 1997.

BIBLIOGRAPHY

Logan, Raford W. "Rayford W. Logan to W. E. B. Du Bois, March 3, 1930." In *The Correspondence of W. E. B. Du Bois*, edited by Herbert Aptheker, 1:420. Amherst: University of Massachusetts Press, 1997.

Lomas, Tim, et al. "The Cryptoterrestrial Hypothesis: A Case for Scientific Openness to a Subterranean Earthly Explanation for Unidentified Anomalous Phenomena." *Philosophy and Cosmology* 33 (2024) 1–42. https://doi.org/10.29202/phil-cosm/33/3.

Long, Charles H. *Ellipsis . . . : The Collected Writings of Charles Long*. London: Bloomsbury, 2018.

———. *Significations: Signs, Symbols, and Images in the Interpretation of Religion*. Aurora, CO: Davies, 1995.

Lopez, Marco. "Olmec Colossal Heads Are of Mesoamerican and Non-African Origin." *Amandala*, Sept. 11, 2021. https://amandala.com.bz/news/olmec-colossal-heads-are-of-mesoamerican-and-non-african-origin/.

Lovejoy, Paul E. "The Context of Enslavement in West Africa: Ahmad Bābā and the Ethics of Slavery." In *Slaves, Subjects, and Subversives: Blacks in Colonial Latin America*, edited by Jane G. Landers and Barry M. Robinson, 9–38. Diálogos. Albuquerque: University of New Mexico Press, 2006.

———. *Transformations in Slavery: A History of Slavery in Africa*. 3rd ed. African Studies 117. Cambridge: Cambridge University Press, 2012.

Lumpkin, Joseph. "Introduction." In *The Negro Bible (The Slave Bible): Select Parts of the Holy Bible, Selected for the Use of the Negro Slaves, in the British West India Islands*, v–xxiv. Blountsville, AL: Fifth Estate, 2019.

Mannix, Daniel P., and Malcolm Cowley. *Black Cargoes: A History of the Atlantic Slave Trade 1518–1865*. New York: Viking, 1962.

Marbury, Herbert Robinson. *Imperial Dominion and Priestly Genius: Coercion, Accommodation, and Resistance in the Divorce Rhetoric of Ezra-Nehemiah*. Upland, CA: Sopher, 2012.

McCray, Walter Arthur. *The Black Presence in the Bible*. 2 vols. Chicago: Black Light Fellowship, 1990.

McDonnell, Wayne M. "Analysis and Assessment of the Gateway Process." CIA, June 9, 1983. https://www.cia.gov/readingroom/docs/cia-rdp96-00788r001700210016-5.pdf.

McGowan, Winston. "The Origins of Slave Rebellions in the Middle Passage." In *The Shadow of the Plantation: Caribbean History and Legacy*, edited by Alvin O. Thompson, 74–99. Kingston: Randle, 2002.

McKittrick, Katherine, ed. "Yours in the Intellectual Struggle: Sylvia Wynter and the Realization of the Living." In *Sylvia Wynter: On Being Human as Praxis*, edited by Katherine McKittrick, 1–89. Durham: Duke University Press, 2015.

McMickle, Marvin A. *Where Have All the Prophets Gone?* Cleveland: Pilgrim, 2006.

McWhorter, John. *Woke Racism: How a New Religion Has Betrayed Black America*. New York: Portfolio, 2021.

Meyer, Marvin, trans. "The Gospel of Thomas with the Greek Gospel of Thomas." In *The Nag Hammadi Scriptures*, edited by Marvin Meyer, 133–56. International ed. New York: Harper One, 2007.

———, ed. *The Nag Hammadi Scriptures*. International ed. New York: Harper One, 2007.

Mignolo, Walter D. "Sylvia Wynter: What Does It Mean to Be Human." In *Sylvia Wynter: On Being Human as Praxis*, edited by Katherine McKittrick, 106–23. Durham: Duke University Press, 2015.

BIBLIOGRAPHY

Mitchell, Henry H. *Black Church Beginnings: The Long-Hidden Realities of the First Years*. Grand Rapids: Eerdmans, 2004.

Moe-Lobeda, Cynthia D. *Resisting Structural Evil*. Minneapolis: Fortress, 2013.

Moore, Richard B. *The Name "Negro": Its Origin and Evil Use*. Edited by W. Burghardt Turner and Joyce Moore Turner. Baltimore: Black Classic, 1992.

Morris, Donald R. *The Washing of the Spears: The Rise and Fall of the Zulu Nation*. New York: Da Capo, 1998.

Morrison, David C. "Pentagon's Top Secret 'Black' Budget Has Skyrocketed During Reagan Years." CIA, Mar. 1, 1986. https://www.cia.gov/readingroom/docs/CIA-RDP90-00965R000504560001-4.pdf.

Morrison, Toni. *The Source of Self-Regard*. New York: Vintage International, 2019.

Mustakeem, Sowande' M. *Slavery at Sea: Terror, Sex, and Sickness in the Middle Passage*. New Black Studies. Urbana: University of Illinois Press, 2017.

Najibi, Alex. "Racial Discrimination in Face Recognition Technology." Harvard University, Oct. 24, 2020. https://projects.iq.harvard.edu/sciencepolicy/blog/racial-discrimination-face-recognition-technology.

Newberg, Andrew, and Mark Robert Waldman. *How God Changes Your Brain: Breakthrough Findings from a Leading Neuroscientist*. New York: Ballantine, 2009.

Nicholl, Don, et al., creators. *The Jeffersons*. Aired Jan. 18, 1975–July 2, 1985, on CBS.

Oden, Thomas C. *How Africa Shaped the Christian Mind: Rediscovering the African Seedbed of Western Christianity*. Early African Christianity. Downers Grove, IL: IVP Academic, 2007.

Otto, Rudolf. *The Idea of the Holy*. Translated by John W. Harvey. New York: Oxford University Press, 1958.

Palmer, Colin A. *Slaves of the White God: Blacks in Mexico, 1570–1650*. Cambridge, MA: Harvard University Press, 1976.

Parfitt, Tudor. *Black Jews in Africa and the Americas*. Nathan I. Huggins Lectures. Cambridge, MA: Harvard University Press, 2013.

Paris, Peter J. *The Social Teaching of the Black Churches*. Philadelphia: Fortress, 1985.

———. *Virtues and Values: The African and African American Experience*. Minneapolis: Fortress, 2004.

Park, Mongo. *Travels into the Interior of Africa*. London: Eland, 2003.

Patterson, Orlando. *The Sociology of Slavery: An Analysis of the Origins, Development, and Structure of Negro Slave Society in Jamaica*. Jamaica: Granada, 1973.

Piketty, Thomas. *Capital in the Twenty-First Century*. Translated by Arthur Goldhammer, Cambridge, MA: Belknap, 2017.

Platt, Rutherford H. *The Lost Books of the Bible and the Forgotten Books of Eden*. New York: One World, 1926.

Poszewiecka, Barbara, et al. "Revised Time Estimation of the Ancestral Human Chromosome 2 Fusion." *BMC Genomics* 23 (2022) 616. https://doi.org/10.1186/s12864-022-08828-7.

Prescod-Weinstein, Chanda. *The Disordered Cosmos: A Journey into Dark Matter, Spacetime, and Dreams Deferred*. New York: Bold Type, 2021.

Ray, Benjamin C. *African Religions: Symbols, Ritual, and Community*. 2nd ed. Upper Saddle River, NJ: Prentice Hall, 2000.

Rediker, Marcus. *The Amistad Rebellion: An Atlantic Odyssey of Slavery and Freedom*. New York: Viking, 2012.

———. *The Slaveship: A Human History*. New York: Penguin, 2007.

BIBLIOGRAPHY

Reis, João José. *Slave Rebellion in Brazil: The Muslim Uprising of 1835 in Bahia*. Translated by Arthur Brakel. Baltimore: Johns Hopkins University Press, 1993.

Restall, Matthew. "Black Conquistadors: Armed Africans in Early Spanish America." *Americas* 57 (2000) 171–205.

Richter, Daniel K. *Before the Revolution: America's Ancient Pasts*. Cambridge, MA: Harvard University Press, 2011.

Robinson, Eugene. *Disintegration: The Splintering of Black America*. New York: Anchor, 2010.

Rodney, Walter. "African Slavery and Other Forms of Social Oppression on the Upper Guinea Coast in the Context of the Atlantic Slave Trade." In *Forced Migration: The Impact of the Export Slave Trade on African Societies*, edited by J. E. Inikori, 61–73. Routledge Library Editions: Slavery. London: Hutchinson University Library, 1982.

Rolfe, John. "John Rolfe's Letter to Sir Edwin Sandys." Salem Press, 1619/1620. Edited by Martha Pallante. Milestone Documents in African American History. https://www.salempress.com/Media/SalemPress/samples/mdaah2_pgs.pdf.

Rudwick, Elliott M. *W. E. B. Du Bois: Propagandist of the Negro Protest*. New York: Atheneum, 1986.

Sanneh, Lamin. *West African Christianity: The Religious Impact*. New York: Orbis, 1983.

Schleiermacher, Friedrich. *On Religion: Speeches to Its Cultured Despisers*. Edited and translated by Richard Crouter. Cambridge: Cambridge University Press, 2006.

Selbie, Joseph. *The Physics of God: How the Deepest Theories of Science Explain Religion and How the Deepest Truths of Religion Explain Science*. Newburyport, MA: New Page, 2021.

Sharpe, Christina. *In the Wake: On Blackness and Being*. Durham: Duke University Press, 2016.

Sigdell, Jan Erik. *Reign of the Anunnaki: The Alien Manipulation of Our Spiritual Destiny*. Rochester, VT: Bear & Co., 2018.

Smallwood, Stephanie E. *Saltwater Slavery: A Middle Passage from Africa to American Diaspora*. Cambridge, MA: Harvard University Press, 2007.

Smith, Connor N. "Outgoing Kentucky Attorney General Named 1792 Exchange CEO." *Spectrum News 1*, Jan. 3, 2024. https://spectrumnews1.com/ky/louisville/news/2024/01/03/kentucky-daniel-cameron-1792-exchange.

Snyder, Timothy. *On Tyranny: Twenty Lessons from the Twentieth Century*. New York: Duggan, 2017.

Soumonni, Elisée. "Lacustrine Villages in South Benin as Refuges from the Slave Trade." In *Fighting the Slave Trade: West African Strategies*, edited by Sylviane A. Diouf, 3–14. Western African Studies. Athens: Ohio University Press, 2003.

Southern, Eileen. *The Music of Black Americans: A History*. 3rd ed. New York: Norton, 1997.

Stallworth, DeWayne R. *Existential Togetherness: Toward a Common Black Religious Heritage*. Eugene, OR: Pickwick, 2019.

Stewart, Maria W. *Maria W. Stewart, America's First Black Woman Political Writer: Essays and Speeches*. Edited by Marilyn Richardson. Bloomington: Indiana University Press, 1987.

Stuckey, Sterling. *Slave Culture: Nationalist Theory and the Foundations of Black America*. 2nd ed. Oxford: Oxford University Press, 2013.

Swanson, David. *War Is a Lie*. 2nd ed. Charlottesville, VA: Just World, 2016.

BIBLIOGRAPHY

Taylor, Eric Robert. *If We Must Die: Shipboard Insurrections in the Era of the Atlantic Slave Trade*. Antislavery, Abolition, and the Atlantic World. Baton Rouge: Louisiana State University Press, 2006.

Taylor, Mark C. *About Religion: Economies of Faith in Virtual Culture*. Religion and Postmodern. Chicago: University of Chicago Press, 1999.

Temple, Robert. *The Sirius Mystery: New Scientific Evidence of Alien Contact 5,000 Years Ago*. Rochester, VT: Destiny, 1998.

Thakur, Tanul. "'Coded Bias' Paints a Terrifying Picture of Facial Recognition's Real Impact on Lives." *Wire*, Apr. 9, 2021. https://thewire.in/film/coded-bias-facial-recognition-ai-netflix-documentary-review.

Thomassen, Einar, and Marvin Meyer, trans. "The Gospel of Truth." In *The Nag Hammadi Scriptures*, edited by Marvin Meyer, 31–47. International ed. New York: Harper One, 2007.

Thompson, Robert Farris. *Flash of the Spirit*. New York: Random House, 1984.

Thornton, John. *Africa and Africans in the Making of the Atlantic World, 1400–1800*. 2nd ed. Studies in Comparative World History. Cambridge: Cambridge University Press, 1998.

———. "Central Africa in the Era of the Slave Trade." In *Slaves, Subjects, and Subversives: Blacks in Colonial Latin America*, edited by Jane G. Landers and Barry M. Robinson, 83–110. Diálogos. Albuquerque: University of New Mexico Press, 2006.

Thurman, Howard. *Jesus and the Disinherited*. New York: Abingdon-Cokesbury, 1949.

Tobin, Jacqueline L., and Dobard G Raymond. *Hidden in Plain View: A Secret Story of Quilts and the Underground Railroad*. New York: Anchor, 2000.

Todorov, Tzvetan. *The Conquest of America: The Question of Other*. Translated by Richard Howard. Norman: University of Oklahoma Press, 1999.

Tyson, Neil deGrasse. *Letters From an Astrophysicist*. New York: Norton & Co., 2019.

Tyson, Neil deGrasse, and Avis Lang. *Accessory to War: The Unspoken Alliance Between Astrophysics and Military*. New York: Norton, 2018.

Van Dantzig, Albert. *Forts and Castles of Ghana*. Accra: Secco, 1999.

Van Sertima, Ivan. *They Came Before Columbus: The African Presence in Ancient America*. New York: Random House, 1976.

Wagner, Roger, and Andrew Briggs. *The Penultimate Curiosity: How Science Swims in the Slipstream of Ultimate Questions*. Oxford: Oxford University Press, 2016.

Walker, David. *David Walker's Appeal: To the Coloured Citizens of the World, but in Particular, and Very Expressly, to Those of the United States of America*. Baltimore: Black Classic, 1993.

Wallace, Mike, and Louis Lomax, producers. *The Hate That Hate Produced*. Aired July 13–17, 1959, on WNTA-TV.

Washington, Michael H., and Cheryl L. Nuñez. "Education, Racial Uplift, and the Rise of the Greek-Letter Tradition: The African American Quest for Status in the Early Twentieth Century." In *African American Fraternities and Sororities: The Legacy and the Vision*, edited by Tamara L. Brown et al., 137–80. Lexington: University Press of Kentucky, 2010.

Watters, Wesley Andrés, et al. "The Scientific Investigation of Unidentified Aerial Phenomena (UAP) Using Multimodal Ground-Based Observatories." *Journal of Astronomical Instrumentation* 12 (2023) 2340006. https://doi.org/10.1142/S2251171723400068.

BIBLIOGRAPHY

Wells, Spencer. *The Journey of Man: A Genetic Odyssey.* Princeton, NJ: Princeton University Press, 2002.

Wildman, Stephanie M., and Adrienne D. Davis. "Making Systems of Privilege Visible." In *White Privilege: Essential Readings on the Other Side of Racism*, edited by Paula S. Rothenburg, 137–43. 5th ed. New York: Worth, 2016.

Wilkerson, Isabel. *Caste: The Origins of Our Discontents.* New York: Random House, 2020.

Wills, Shomari. *Black Fortunes: The Story of the First Six African Americas Who Survived Slavery and Became Millionaires.* New York: Amistad, 2019.

Wilmore, Gayraud S. *Black Religion and Black Radicalism: An Examination of the Black Experience in Religion.* New York: Anchor Doubleday, 1973.

———. *Pragmatic Spirituality: The Christian Faith Through an Afrocentric Lens.* New York: New York University Press, 2004.

Wimbush, Vincent L. "We Will Make Our Own Future Text: An Alternate Orientation to Interpretation." In *True to Our Native Land: An African American New Testament Commentary*, edited by Brian K. Blount et al., 43–53. Minneapolis: Fortress, 2007.

Winters, Clyde A. "The Nubians and Olmecs." Olmec 98, n.d. https://olmec98.net/ortiz1.htm. Site discontinued.

———. "Skeletal Evidence of African Olmecs in Ancient America." Olmec 98, n.d. https://olmec98.net/Skeletal.htm. Site discontinued.

Wood, Peter H. *Black Majority: Negroes in Colonial South Carolina from 1670 through the Stono Rebellion.* Norton Library. New York: Norton, 1974.

Woodson, Carter G. *The Negro in Our History.* Washington, DC: Associated, 1922.

Wynter, Sylvia, and Katherine McKittrick. "Unparalleled Catastrophe for Our Species? Or, to Give Humanness a Different Future: Conversations." In *Sylvia Wynter: On Being Human as Praxis*, edited by Katherine McKittrick, 9–89. Durham: Duke University Press, 2015.

Yehuda, Rachel. "How Parents' Trauma Leaves Biological Traces in Children." *Scientific American*, July 1, 2022. https://www.scientificamerican.com/article/how-parents-rsquo-trauma-leaves-biological-traces-in-children/.

York, Michael. *Pagan Theology: Paganism as a World Religion.* New York: NYU Press, 2005.

Young, Jason R. *Rituals of Resistance: African Atlantic Religion in Kongo and the Lowcountry South in the Era of Slavery.* Baton Rouge: Louisiana State University Press, 2007.

INDEX

Abuka, Edmund, 54–55n31
adinkra codes, 13
african american cultural ethos, 68
african collective spirit, 98
african drums, 95
african europeans, 38, 40
ancient orientation of consciousness, 127
african religious/spiritual leader, 102
african tribalism, 92
afro-portugese, 39
akan peoples, 41
Allport's five-point scale of extermination, 3n2
amma, 13
amistad, 93–94
ancient blackness, 22
ankh, 34
annunnaki, 24
Antonio, the negro, 46
Arbery, Ahmaud, 9, 11
archimedean, 107
Armstrong, Louis, 29
artificial intelligence (ai), 122–24
atlantic creoles/cousins, 40, 45
atlantic islands, 50
atra-hasis, 23
aum/om, 18
authentic spiritualists, 126–27

Baartman, Sarah, 4
Baquaqua, Mahommah Gardo, 61
barracoons, 58, 64
Barrett, Amy Comey, 31
batiments of haiti, 62

beasts of burden, 49
bell hooks, 81
Bibb, Henry, 45
big bang, 12–13, 18
bigotry, reflection on, 19n20
bindedness, 63
black as a cultural phenomenon, 58, 66
black church, the inception of, 92n1
black commodities, 42
black conquistadors, 56n40
black codes, 6
black cultural oppression, 67
black gold, 60
blacks hybrid, 115n19
black intellectual, 7
black intellectualism and social assimilation, 10n3
black jesus, 66
black jews, 12n6
black lived experience, 58, 65, 68, 70–71, 73–74, 76
black lives matter, 29
black nationalism, 69
black plague, 50
black privilege, 67, 71, 73–74
black privilege, Spike Lee's cultural analysis of, 35n8
black psyche, 71
black religion and rebellion, 100n50
black skin othering, 3–6, 65, 71, 107, 129, 5n5, 68n4, 108n3, 110n3
black social analysis of survival, 105
black sub-world, 40, 67–68, 77
black zeitgeist, 29–30, 65–67, 70, 73
bobangi, 44

INDEX

bondedness, necessity of, 63
Booker, Cory 31
book of enoch, 23
Bradley, Justice Joseph 73
brown fellowship society, 45
Brown, John, 67
Bruno, Giordano 114
buddhist religious tradition, 127
Byrd Jr., James, 27–29

cabildos, 98
camarada, 98
Cameron, Daniel 32
cameronian pleasure, 32
canoe experience, 58n1
Capitein, Johannes Eliza, 40
chattel enslavement, 4
christ consciousness, 118, 125–26
Cinque, 93
civil war, 118
civil rights act of 1875, 6
coalesced hybrid blacks, 7, 115, 130
coded bias, 122
code switch, 70
Coleman, C. D., 104
compromising hybrid blacks, 39
compromising slave preacher, 102
Cone, James, 65
consciousness, 7, 113, 129–30
coromantee, 41–42
cosmic blackness, 18
cosmic conscious intelligence, 19
cosmos, 14, 18, 126–28, 130
creole, 94
crisis, 107
Cruse, Harold, 10
cultural connection to tradition, 126
cultural metaphor of identity, 105
cultural privileging, 21
cultural points of departure, 49n8

dark energy, 19
darpa (defense advanced research project agency), 120
day of the fish, 22, 25
day of the lord, 25
death march, 58
dirty black hand, 2

divine spark within, 127
dna and cloning, 19–20, 24
domestics, 45
dogon, 20, 13, 22
dogon/akan error-correcting codes, 13
Douglas Kelly, Brown, 65
Du Bois, W. E. B., 5, 10, 25, 26, 35, 60, 76–77, 80–89, 103, 107–12
duboisian social categorization, 85n27
dyula, 49

early african religious practices, 99n49
early relations between africans and europeans, 53n23
early slave submission politics, 68
Einstein, Albert, 112, 16–118
Eisenhower, Dwight, 119
elitism, 68
Enlil, 24
Enki, Ea, 23–24
enuma elish, 13, 24
epic of gilamesh, 23
Equiano, Olaudah, 62
eshu (spirit of individuality and change), 199
european psyche, 4
existential crisis for africans, 99
existential togetherness, 71–72, 92, 102
eye of god, 117

Falconbridge, Alexander, 62
Fanon, Frantz, 8, 35, 81–82
first slave trading corporations, 55n23
first wave of the african enslaved, 99n48
Floyd, George Jr., 28–29, 69
Franklin, John Hope, 60
Frazier, E Franklin, 68, 103
Freud, Sigmund, 78
fulas, 43
fuxi, 22

Gates, Sylvester James, 13
gift of god, 59
Goddess Tiamat, 13
Gomez, Michael, 63
gondwanaland, 16
great compromise, 9n11

INDEX

great dismal swamp, 94
grimaldi man, 15
gucumatz, 13
Guerrero, Vicente, 17

Harding, Vincent, 60
hate that hate produced, 69
His holiness the dalai lama, 126b
Holiday, Billie, 70
Holloway, Joseph, 59
homo erectus, 23
homo denisovans, 23
homo floresienis, 23
homo neanderthalensis, 23
homo narran, 12
homo sapiens, 23
hooks, bell, 81
Horowitz, David, 73
human brutality, 13n3
human manifestation of a supernatural force, 81n10
human need for religious meaning, 79n7
human soul, 131
Hurston, Zora Neale, 61
hybrid black, 7, 8, 39–40, 46, 117, 125

ifa, (god of divination), 100
infinite source, 130
instructors, 22
isthus of suez, 15
Itanko, 62
ivory tower, 11
Iyan, 13

james webb space telescope (jwst), 19
jeffersons, 90
jewish cultural politics, 126
Jim Crow, 6, 67, 71–71, 117, 125

King, Anu, 24
King, Martin Luther Jr., 6, 66, 104–6, 112–15, 119
kingian rhetoric, 125
kootoo, 94
krumen, 44

laws of eshunna, 77
laws of hammurabi, 77

legalism, 77
Lewis, Cudjo, 61
Lincoln, Abraham, 67
Lincoln, C. Eric, 105
Long, Charles, 24n41, 61
Logan, Rayford, 5

mande, 16
mandinka slatees, 43
Malcom X, 69
malungo of Brazil, 62
mandingos, 43
manifest destiny, 81
Marduk, 13, 25
masters of the sea, 22
mati of surinam, 62
McIntosh, Peggy, 73
McWhorter, John, 33–35
mesoamerica culture, 15–17
middle passage, 63, 100
military-industrial complex (mic), 119
Mitchell, Henry, 103
monitors, 22
moors, 48
morbid class consciousness, 104
Mutwa, Credo, 20
myth, 12
myth of black, 12
mysterium tremendum, 117

n.a a.c.p, 107
nation of islam, 69
national defense authorization act, 119
negritude, 11
negro act of 1740, 97
new world, 3–4, 7, 9, 25, 30, 39, 43–44, 46–48, 50–51, 53–54, 56–57, 62, 64,–65, 71, 73, 78–80, 94, 99–100, 106, 113–16
new world economic system, 37–38
new world plantation systems, 14
new world slavery, 30
Nicholas, Tyre, 70–71
Nimrod, 23
Ninhasak, 24
nine rules of survival, 90
nommo (s), 22
nubians, 16

INDEX

obeah, 100–101
occult traditions, 126
ogo, 13
ogun (god of iron), 100
Old Doll, 45
Olmec, 15–17
olorun, 13
oshoosi (god of hunting), 100
oshun (goddess of beauty and water), 100
other, 2, 9, 14, 32, 81, 83, 128
otherness, 4, 27, 76, 81, 86
othering, 35, 71, 82, 118
owa coco, 61
origin of the cosmos, 20
origin of the human, 13n1
orishas, 13

partus sequitur ventrem, 52
piccaninni sestus, 43
plessy v. ferguson, 6
poisoning, 97
politics of the corporate academy, 8
polyvalent nature of African peoples, 63n29
poro and sande, 93
practice of African sand eating, 106n74
psychological wage, 89
(1619) project, 9n10
Punch, John, 5

quilombos, 98

religiously legitimated society, 76n1
religion of the american negro, 46n46
religion of whiteness, 35, 76, 79–81, 84–85, 87
romanus pontifex, 51

san juan bautista, 5
Scott, Dred, 88
Schleirmacher, Fredrich, religious formations of, 79n6
second temple priesthood, 78
Sertima, Ivan Van 15–17
seti (the search for extraterrestrial intelligence), 121
sexual assaults, 62
siccadingers, 43

sirius system, 20
sky people, 13
slave bible, 44
slave preachers, 102
slave ship rebellions, 93n5
slave consciousness, 72
social construction, 31n4
social division, the crux of, 82n14
social isolation, 104
social stratification, 67, 69
social structure, 78n3
sorrow songs, 92
speculum orsis, 97
Stewart, Maria, 80
stono rebels, 96
Stuckey, Sterling, 61, 63n30
sub-stratification of elitism, 68
sub-world, 115
sumerian blackheads, 23
supreme olorun, 100
susus, 43

Telemachus, 44
tepeu, 13
Tesla, Nikola, 127
Thornton, John, 60
thing, 6, 26–27, 29, 35–36, 107–9, 11, 112–14, 119, 124
Tha God, Charlamagne, 74
the souls of white folk, 85
the philadelphia negro, 10
the souls of black folk, 10
Thurman, Howard, 7
Till, Emmett, 28n2
traditional black preacher, 106
traditional religion, 126
transformation of black skin, 52n19
trauma of the slave ship, 60n8
treaty of tordesillas, 51
Turner, Henry M., 103
Turner, Nat, 102, 115
typical slave ship, 59n4
Tyson, Neil Degrasse, 32–33

uncoalesed hybrid blacks, 7, 115
uncoalesced hybrid black scholar, 11
uncompromisinsg hybrid blacks, 39, 41
uncompromising enslaved africans, 71

INDEX

unified oneness of black skin, 59
unified slave consciousness, 72
us army intelligence command, 121

vietnam, 113
veil, 76
vera cruz, 16
vodun, 99–100

Walker, David, 45n41
watchdogs, 7, 38, 41–42
Weinstein-Prescod, Chanda., 18

whiteness, 35, 74, 76, 84, 87–88, 74, 76
white gaze of retaliation, 70
white lion, 5
white privilege, 88, 90–91
white racial frame, 89
Winters, Clyde 16
wokeness, 34–35
Wynter, Sylvia, 12

yemoja (goddess of the seas), 100

zulu myth of mars, 20n24

www.ingramcontent.com/pod-product-compliance
Lightning Source LLC
Chambersburg PA
CBHW031459160426
43195CB00010BB/1027